Country Walks
near London

Country Walks near London

52 walks within easy reach of the capital

CHRISTOPHER SOMERVILLE

SIMON & SCHUSTER

LONDON·SYDNEY·NEW YORK·TOKYO·SINGAPORE·TORONTO

First published in Great Britain by
Simon & Schuster Ltd in 1994
A Paramount Communications Company

Simon & Schuster Ltd
West Garden Place
Kendal Street
London W2 2AQ

Simon & Schuster of Australia Pty Ltd
Sydney

A CIP catalogue record for this book is
available from the British Library
ISBN 0–671–71264–0

Typeset by Florencetype Ltd, Kewstoke, Avon
Printed and bound in Great Britain by
The Bath Press, London and Bath

*For my sisters Julia and Louisa,
and all other Londoners
longing for a breath of fresh air*

Acknowledgements

I would like to thank Clive King of Luton & District Transport, Simon Archer of County Bus & Coach, Alex Pavitt of Kentish Bus & Coach and Stephen Salmon of London & Country Buses for their help. I'm also grateful to Carol and Rosalind O'Brien for suggesting walks.

ONE HOUR FROM NOW . . .

Are you sweltering in a rush-hour tube tunnel between Oxford Circus and Marble Arch as you read these words, or jostling in a jampacked bookshop in the Charing Cross Road at lunchtime? Perhaps you have collapsed into a Docklands Light Railway train at the end of a hard day, or are sitting with a pint of beer in a pub in Kentish Town. Wherever in overcrowded, built-up London you are at this minute, reader, an hour from now you could be taking your first step on one of the exhilarating country walks waiting for you between the covers of this book.

Imagine it: treading a path that winds through ancient beechwoods splashed with autumn reds and golds in the rolling Chiltern Hills; admiring rows of apple trees in full blossom in a springtime Kentish orchard; gulping the bracing wind of a wintry Essex salt-marsh thronged with wildfowl; relaxing in the garden of a country pub in summer sunshine at the end of a breezy stroll across the Surrey downs.

These 52 walks – one for each weekend of the year – are scattered round the rim of London. You can reach all but a handful from central London by public transport, most of them within an hour or so. There's an astonishing range of peaceful countryside within easy reach of the city, and this book is the key to it. You don't need to be a dedicated footslogger to enjoy these walks – most can be managed comfortably in two or three hours by the least energetic of weekend ramblers, and several have short cuts indicated which save you a mile or two. You don't need any equipment more forbidding than a stout pair of walking shoes. But do take the relevant Ordnance Survey 1:50,000 Landranger map recommended in the information box of each walk.

Clear instructions and maps are included to get you from central London to the start, to guide you round the walk and bring you back to your starting point. There are notes on all kinds of interesting features along the way – wildlife, local legends and tall stories, ancient churches, fine houses, good pubs and suggestions for reading to help you enjoy your ramble to the full.

Some of the walks are set in well-known locations – the venerable woods of Burnham Beeches in Buckinghamshire and Epping Forest in Essex, for example, or Berkshire's royal parklands at Windsor Castle. Even in these popular spots you will quickly find yourself out of sight and sound of other people. Most walks, however, are in deep, quiet countryside ripe for exploration; while some – especially those a little further away, out in the eastern marshlands – will take you where you will have only sea winds and bird calls for company.

You'll discover Saxon chapels like St Peter's-on-the-Wall in remotest Essex, and Norman churches like St Thomas's, marooned on the loneliest tip of the Isle of Sheppey in Kent; historic houses such as Chenies in the Chilterns, Shaw's Corner in Hertfordshire and the moated Elizabethan mansion of Crowhurst Place in Surrey; the ancient trackways of the Ridgeway, the Icknield Way and the Pilgrim's Way, trodden since prehistoric times; heathlands in Surrey and coppice woods in Buckinghamshire and Essex linked far more strongly to bygone centuries than this one.

Above all, you'll exchange London and its traffic-laden streets, its barging and pushing, its workaday worries, its man-made environment, for a few hours of fresh air, wide horizons and natural surroundings. You'll return to the city with something memorable to savour in retrospect, and the prospect of more to look forward to next weekend.

I wish you a wonderful country walk from London – 52 times over.

Christopher Somerville

· CONTENTS ·

Contents

Contents

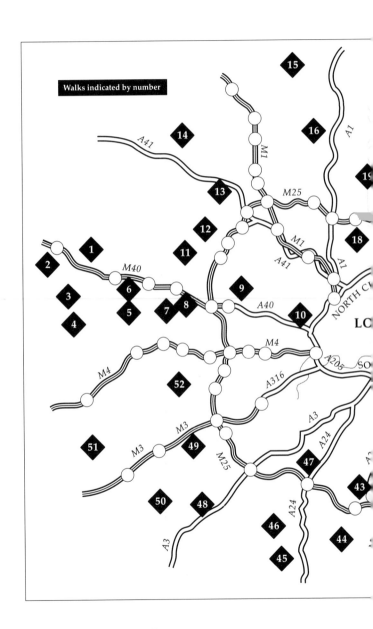

Walks indicated by number

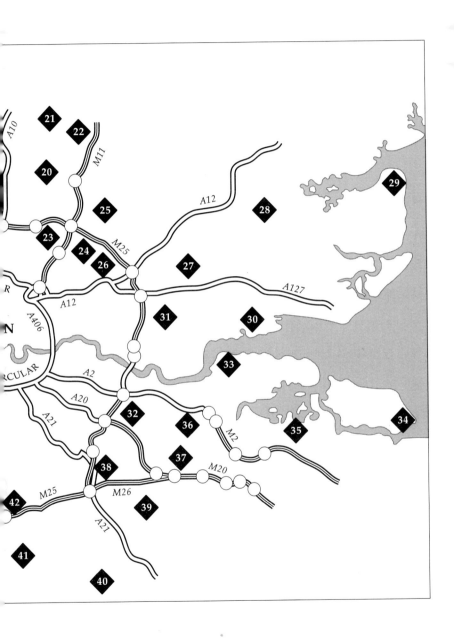

GETTING THERE . . .

Although most of these walks are easily accessible by public transport, it is vital to check up well in advance on bus and train times, to avoid disappointment on the day of your walk. Remember – bus services in the remoter country districts may be rather threadbare at weekends.

Rural Britain is, on the whole, poorly served by buses, and the countryside round London is no exception. However, the excellent Green Line bus services from Victoria Coach Station and other pick-up points in central London will get you to most towns and many villages near the walks. Where possible I have listed the routes and stops. Do let me know if you discover bus routes I haven't listed.

The County Councils of Bucks, Herts, Essex, Kent and Surrey operate telephone information services (9–5, Monday to Friday as a rule) which will provide you with accurate, up-to-date information on local services within their respective counties. The information section of those walks accessible by bus includes the relevant phone number, as well as the Green Line main information number (081 668–7261) to help you plan your bus journey from central London. For the handful of walks in Oxfordshire and Berkshire, the appropriate bus company number is given.

Green Line itself has recently split into four parts, and further information can be obtained from them if necessary, as well as bus maps and timetables. They are:

1. LUTON & DISTRICT TRANSPORT (Berks, Bucks and West Herts), Tavistock Street, Dunstable, Beds LU6 1NE.
Area telephone numbers for information:
Aylesbury – 0296 23445
Hemel Hempstead – 0442 216934
High Wycombe – 0494 464647
Hitchin – 0462 434132
Luton – 0582 404074
Slough – 0753 575275

2. COUNTY BUS & COACH COMPANY (East Herts and Essex), Fourth Avenue, Harlow, Essex CM20 1DU. Tel: 0279 421971

3. KENTISH BUS & COACH COMPANY (Kent), Apex House, London Road, Northfleet, Kent DA11 9PD. Tel: 0474 325533

4. LONDON & COUNTRY BUSES (Surrey, Sussex), Lesbourne Road, Reigate, Surrey RH2 7LE. Tel: 0737 242411

...AND ON THE TRAIL

I have covered every mile of these walks on foot while writing this book, and have taken trouble to get the route instructions as accurate as possible. But things change continually in the countryside, and by the time you set out there may have been small alterations to signposts, stiles, shapes of orchards and so on. I would be delighted to receive information from readers about such changes as they occur, and will incorporate them into future editions. If you have any other comments or recommendations, these will also be very gratefully received and acknowledged.

Hearnton Wood
and West Wycombe
(Bucks)

INFORMATION

Map OS 1:50,000 Landranger Sheets 165 'Aylesbury and
Leighton Buzzard'; 175 'Reading and Windsor'.

Travel

> TRAIN (BR) – Saunderton station.
>
> CAR – M40 to Jct 4; A4010. Park at station.
>
> BUS – Green Line (Victoria) 081 668–7261. Local infor-
> mation: 0296 382000. London Victoria–High Wycombe–
> Saunderton: bus stops at Golden Cross PH on A4010,
> 200 yards from Saunderton BR station.

Length of walk 7½ miles – circular – start and finish at
Saunderton station (✄ *short cut* – 6 miles).

Conditions Woodland tracks; field paths; short stretch of A41
(grass verge).

Opening times

> *St Lawrence's Church, West Wycombe* Sundays, sometimes
> Saturdays.
>
> *West Wycombe Caves* May–mid September, Monday–Friday,
> 11–6. Late September, October, March, April, 1–6.
> March–October, Sundays, Bank Holidays, 11–6.
>
> *West Wycombe House Grounds* April and May, Sundays and
> Wednesdays 2–6; Easter, May and Spring Bank Holidays,
> 2–6. House and grounds June, July, August, Sundays–
> Thursdays 2–6.

Refreshments Golden Cross, Saunderton (on A4010); George and
Dragon or Old Plough, High Street, West Wycombe.

At the heart of this walk in the western Chilterns is the picturesque
village of West Wycombe, where in the 1750s Sir Francis Dashwood –
part rake-hell, part conscientious squire – ran his notorious Hellfire
Club in the caves under the hill on whose slopes he built a great folly of
a mausoleum. At the summit he topped St Lawrence's Church with a
club room inside a golden globe for wild parties – or so the stories say.

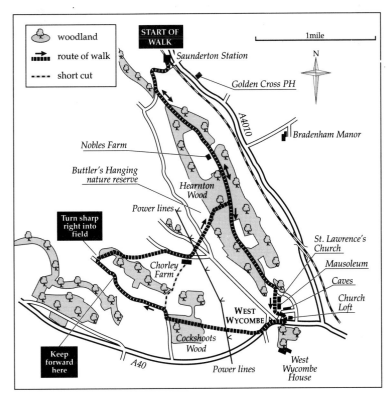

You'll also enjoy long stretches of lonely walking through beech woods, and an ancient track running past a beautiful Elizabethan farmstead.

From Saunderton station (813981) walk down the station approach road and turn right up the road, round a left-hand hair-pin bend and, in 150 yards, left up a track marked 'Nobles Farm' (811977 – footpath sign). The track leaves the rolling cornfield landscape to climb past old holly and yew trees, its banks thick with bellflowers, to run along the ridge under the ash and beech trees of Hearnton Wood, where in just over a mile it passes the flint and brick house and converted barns of Nobles Farm, built in 1725 (819968). Beyond the farm the view to the left opens out over the big red block of Bradenham Manor (829971), a superb squirearchical picture as it dominates the little grey church and neat roadside cottages of Bradenham. Benjamin Disraeli, prime minister and novelist of the Victorian era, grew up here.

One and a half miles beyond Nobles Farm, the golden globe on the tower of St Lawrence's Church begins to peep over the trees ahead, and soon the path runs to the left of the church. Bear right across an open grassy space to reach the church (827950) and the

mausoleum just below it. Steep steps lead down the slope to the right, bearing left at the bottom to reach the caves (829948) and the village of West Wycombe below.

St Lawrence's was rebuilt in flint by Sir Francis Dashwood in the 1750s, and furnished with the circular golden club room where up to a dozen Hellfire Club members could 'play cards', as more polite accounts put it. The chains that shackle the globe to the corners of the tower, and the little round portholes in its sides, increase its resemblance to a bathysphere anchored on some sea floor. 'The best Globe Tavern I ever drunk in,' said John Wilkes, club member and campaigner for the rights of individuals. Inside the church the decorations – Italianate, baroque, fantastical – reflect Dashwood's interest in classical and other forms of architecture. Whether the church was ever the setting for Black Masses is open to conjecture; likewise the hexagonal, open-topped mausoleum on the hillside below, its niches holding stone urns said to have been placed there to receive the hearts of Hellfire members. Massive, cold and empty, it looks more like a rich man's folly than a fiendish venue – in the broad light of day, that is.

The modern display in the caves gives a good idea of what the members of the Hellfire Club (many of them ministers of state, all of them influential people) got up to in the 1750s and 60s – drinking, gambling, fornicating, dressing up. Much the same as today, in fact. Dashwood himself was not as black as he was painted – he excavated the caves for material to surface the local roads, and produced a new Prayer Book for 'young and lively' people. Probably he was just a rich, intelligent man with too much time on his hands.

The village is delightful, all in brick and timber, carefully preserved by the National Trust. The 15th-century Church Loft on the High Street (830947), where in former times the churchwardens met, has a tiny prison cell in its archway and a stone in the foundations of its western end hollowed by the knees of those praying under the crucifix whose empty receptacle is still imprinted in the beam above. Every building in the High Street is full of charm; but the A41 tortures West Wycombe, coating its historic buildings with grime – an excellent incentive to bypass the village, or better still ban traffic entirely from its streets.

Leave the village along the A41 Stokenchurch road, turning right in 150 yards over a stile (825946) to follow white arrows under power lines, uphill across two fields and into Cockshoots Wood over another stile (817947). White splashes on the tree trunks lead you ¼ mile to turn right up a flinty path on leaving the wood (813947). In 50 yards bear left at a fork in the path (✂ *short cut* – keep straight on to Chorley Farm), walking between open fields across the crest of an 'island' of ground surrounded by valleys. Keep forward where the track doglegs right into a farmyard

(806952), through a metal gateway on the left in 50 yards, then a wooden one (white arrow) to rejoin the track beyond the farm and continue to the junction of Hatch Lane and Green End Road on a sharp bend (803954).

Turn right, then immediately right again into a field (footpath sign), turning left with the hedge and road on your left, and follow the field edge down and round to the right. Where the trees turn uphill, turn left (805955) downhill through the wood. The path bears right and runs along the bottom of the wood to a stile (807955 – white arrow), then crosses two fields. This stretch of the walk is an ancient trackway that reaches a road (813955) where you turn right to reach Chorley Farm (815954) (✄ *short cut* – rejoins). The farm house is Elizabethan, a harmonious cream-and-black building whose timber framing was made in part of old ships' timbers. Opposite the farm a stile (white arrow; footpath No. 9) points you uphill with a fence on your left, under power lines to cross two lanes into the valley bottom (817958). Cross the lane and climb steeply up the hillside, slanting left across Buttler's Hanging nature reserve to enter Hearnton Wood through a gate on the crest of the ridge (819960).

The sheep-nibbled chalk grassland of Buttler's Hanging is rich in all kinds of wildlife – wild thyme, rockrose, vetches, yellow-wort, orchids, wild candytuft, the rare purple Chiltern gentian; small, common and chalkhill blue butterflies; many kinds of spider, some rare. The patches of scrub include dogwood, sweet briar and the shrub-like wayfaring tree with its black and red berries, while the taller grassland supports knapweed, scabious and marjoram, where the great green bush cricket lives. This is a little treasury of wild plants and animals, carefully watched and warded by the Naturalists' Trusts of Berks, Bucks and Oxfordshire.

Walk up through the trees, crossing a path and continuing over the crown of the ridge to meet the track (821962) where you turn left for Nobles Farm and Saunderton station.

2

Watlington Hill, Blackmoor Wood and Christmas Common
(Oxfordshire)

INFORMATION

Map OS 1:50,000 Landranger Sheet 175 'Reading and Windsor'.
Travel CAR – M40 to Jct 6; B4009 to Watlington; left turn in
centre of the village on to Hill Road to Christmas Common.
Length of walk 7 miles – circular – start and finish at National
Trust car park on Watlington Hill (✂ *short cut* – 3½ miles).
Conditions Chalk and flint tracks, much in woodland, two short
nasty sections of road. Take tree book.
Refreshments Fox and Hounds, Christmas Common.
Reading Oxfordshire Country Walks Vol 2 – Chilterns by Mary
Webb, Alan Spicer and Allister Smith (Oxfordshire Books)
Walks 3 and 4.

Walking among the beechwoods on the west-facing escarpment of the
Chiltern hills, you can enjoy the twin pleasures of tremendous views
over the Oxfordshire plain to the west, and the serene silence of the
woods with their network of leaf-strewn chalk tracks. Old pastureland
now partly grown with woodland, aromatic with wild herbs and
studded with ancient trees, sloping and climbing above the plain, gives
the keynote to this memorable walk from Christmas Common, with a
superb old-fashioned pub to round things off.

**Footpaths and bridleways radiate out from the National Trust car
park on the crest of Watlington Hill (709936). Turn right out of
the car park entrance along the road for 40 yards, then right again
along the south-east edge of the car park into a tunnel of trees,
following white arrow waymarks on tree trunks and 'W7' path
numbers. The great beeches of this woodland overhang the path as
it drops downhill through a kissing gate, at first in the light green
shade of the beeches and then in the more sombre shadow of
gnarled old yew trees.**

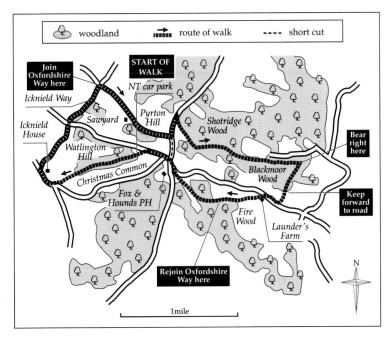

These yews were growing here centuries before the once open common land of Christmas Common was enclosed and the beeches began to flourish. Christmas Common was named, so the old story goes, after a truce arranged on Christmas Day 1643 between local Royalists and Parliamentarians during the Civil War. A more prosaic, but maybe more likely, explanation is that it got its name from the Oxfordshire peasants' word for the holly trees that still grow plentifully hereabouts – the 'Christmas Tree'.

At the foot of the hill (696930) turn right along the B480 Watlington road for a short and nasty 300 yards, round a sharp right-hand bend to pass Icknield House and turn right up the Icknield Way (694932).

The ancient Icknield Way, used by travellers since Stone Age times, runs here under the name of the Ridgeway path. It's a narrow flint and chalk track between thick hedges that have grown here since early medieval times – spindle bushes and wild service trees, indicators of ancient hedgerows, bear witness to that. The path crosses the Watlington–Christmas Common road (698940) and widens, a broad old highway curling round the feet of the downs, hedged here with yew, its verges bright with yellow ragwort and purple feathery knapweed.

In ⅓ mile the track meets the Oxfordshire Way long distance footpath (703945), and here you turn right and commence a long climb up Pyrton Hill, with the resinous scent of a saw yard on your right (708940) growing fainter as the path rises up the flank of a dry, scrubby valley.

Pyrton Hill, like Christmas Common, was enclosed in the mid-19th century, and became covered in scrub as the commoners ceased grazing their sheep on its slopes. But the old grassland herbs still grow – marjoram, basil, thyme – scenting the air. The Oxfordshire Way hereabouts was once known as Knightsbridge Lane, an ancient track whose ribbony, dust-grey course can be seen from Pyrton Hill snaking away into the plain. Rabbits burrow the loose soil, and roe deer flash across the path into the thorn bushes.

Near the top of the hill, footpath PY1 runs off temptingly to the right, but keep straight ahead to the road (715937) (✄ *short cut* – turn right to Christmas Common), where you turn left for 400 yards round a sharp right-hand bend; then immediately right onto a footpath (715940 – footpath fingerpost) through the southern outskirts of Shotridge Wood. 250 yards past a clearing among the beech trees (717936) the path divides: a forked white arrow on a tree trunk shows path PY3 running off to the right, while SH4 diverges to the left. Ignore them and keep straight ahead for 150 yards beside the edge of the wood, where a white arrow points decisively to the left, downhill along a narrow path for a mile and more.

Shotridge Wood – which soon becomes Blackmoor Wood as you descend – was also once open pastureland. The tall, slender beeches have grown well on the old grazing slopes, each racing its neighbours to put on height and reach the sunlight in a burst of vegetation fifty feet up, an effect like tropical rain forest. The smooth-barked trunks shine in the slanting sunlight with a richly luminous, silver-grey glow, as if lit from inside. Further down into the wood the path passes a 'Wormsley Estate' notice among shorter, more scrubby woodland of hazel, goat willow and crab apple – all trees that show where the damp bottom of the valley was open to the sky and the teeth of sheep before the beech trees invaded.

Just before joining a forest road (736935) bear right (bent white arrow) and in 100 yards go right uphill (white arrow marked SH8), inside the edge of the wood. After 300 yards the track swings round to the left; don't follow it, but put your trust in the white arrows on trees to the right of the bend, which point diagonally uphill to the right, a steep climb that brings you out on to overgrown common land at the top of the wood (732929). Go straight forward to

reach the road, where you turn right for 400 yards to reach a cluster of houses. A green public bridleway sign (728929), just before a wooden bus shelter and an old silver-painted Bucks/Oxfordshire county boundary marker, points to the left here.

The path enters the grounds of Launders Farm to the right of a brick shed, and crosses fields over five stiles in succession (white arrow waymarks). The fifth stile takes you into Fire Wood (724928), still following white arrows, to bear right along the Oxfordshire Way (722927) to a junction of tracks and a confusing mass of arrows and path numbers. Snake to the left here, following OW/PS3 signs, to turn right up a flinty track (718928) and reach the road at Christmas Common. Keep straight ahead (though the excellent, unspoilt Fox and Hounds lies only a few yards down the Nettlebed road) to turn left along the Watlington road (714934) (✂ *short cut* – rejoins) and regain the car park on Watlington Hill – but not before enjoying a final gaze over the stretching miles of the Oxfordshire plain laid out before you.

3

Hambleden, Skirmett
and Great Wood
(Bucks)

INFORMATION

Map OS 1:50,000 Landranger Sheet 175 'Reading and Windsor'.
Travel CAR – M40 to Jct 4; A404; A4155 through Marlow
   towards Henley. Hambleden turn is on the right, 4 miles west
   of Marlow. Park behind Stag and Huntsman.
Length of walk 7½ miles – circular – start and finish at
   Hambleden church.
Conditions Well-trodden field paths; woodland paths and
   tracks.
Refreshments Stag and Huntsman, Hambleden; Old Crown or
   King's Head, Skirmett.
Reading Notes at St Mary's Church, Hambleden.

This is a tale of two villages – Hambleden, the charming National Trust village with a vigorous life, much visited, a lively little place; and Skirmett, also charming in appearance, but with every one of its village amenities (except for two good pubs) pared away by 20th-century commuterism. The walk runs up the peaceful Hambleden valley that connects the two places, returning above the valley through the winding ways of Great Wood.

Hambleden sits contentedly round its triangular 'square'; village shop, upmarket Stag and Huntsman Inn, diminutive garage, cottages of flint and brick with roses round their porches and creepers on their walls. The butcher's shop, now closed, still has its hand-painted sign. Only the cars look out of place. The church sits facing the village centre; the squire's house peeps out of trees beyond. Hambleden is one of those just-so Chiltern villages.

St Mary's Church is a gem, a large cruciform flint building. Inside is a striking tub font that may predate the Normans, carved with crosses shaped like flying swallows. In the chancel the 14th-century triple sedilia or priest's seat is decorated with three faces carved in chalk, so expressive and sharp in detail one can hardly believe they are over 600

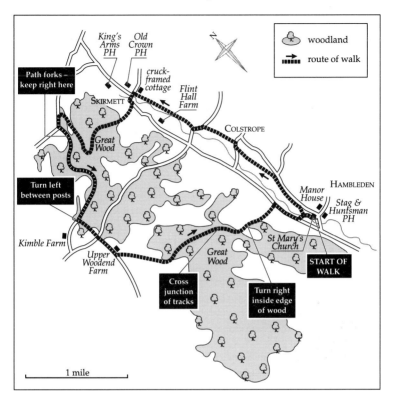

years old. Next to the south transept, the Lady Chapel was once known as the 'sheepfold' when besmocked farm labourers were corralled here to kneel in straw, away from finer folk. The south transept contains an altar fronted by intricate 14th-century carving in glowing dark wood – pontiffs and prelates, a tiny Virgin and Child, strange combatants in flat caps mounted on unlikely beasts and waving clubs at each other – said to have formed the headboard of a bed where Cardinal Wolsey once slept: his arms are incorporated in the carving. In the north transept is a notable alabaster monument to Sir Cope D'Oyley (died 1633), his wife Martha ('Prudently simple, providently wary/To the world a Martha and to heaven a Mary') and their ten children, the four who died young holding skulls. Here also stands the oak chest taken to the Crimea by James Brudenell, Lord Cardigan, who commanded the Charge of the Light Brigade in 1854 – he was born at the Manor House, and baptised in the Saxon font.

From the church lych gate (783865) turn right up the lane, and in 250 yards go right through a kissing gate before a little bridge (782868) to cross a field, aiming for the last house along the road. Here you join the path running north through the Hambleden

valley, a wide hollow of fields and woods, calm and quiet, dotted with handsome farmhouses. At Colstrope you join a road for 100 yards beside a square flint farmhouse with big old barns and sheds (782881), to continue along the path at a public bridleway sign, guided by white arrows, past the harmonious cluster of buildings at Flint Hall Farm, to reach a road at Skirmett (777899).

Up the lane to the right is an ancient cottage, bowed under tiled roof and zig-zag chimneys, the arched end beams of its medieval cruck frame clearly visible.

Turn left, then right at the road to stroll along the single street of the village.

The street is lined with pretty houses in a beautiful setting, but with an all-too-familiar story to be read in their names. Here are the Old School, the Old Forge and the Old Post Office, all now converted to houses. Beyond them the old church and chapel have been likewise metamorphosed, as have the weatherboarded, long-windowed butcher's, the slaughterhouse and the cobbler's. Skirmett has become a commuter village, to which incomers return at night and from which they depart early in the morning. They buzz to High Wycombe or Marlow in their cars for shopping. In the past couple of decades Skirmett has lost every one of its amenities – even the bus has all but ceased calling.

One 'Old' in Skirmett has retained its life, however – the Old Crown pub, where you can enjoy excellent food and local beer under a forest of china sauce-boats, hanging from the beams – unless you prefer the King's Arms up the street.

From the Old Crown turn left, back the way you came, to follow the road as it bends right and left; then turn immediately right over a stile (775898 – footpath sign) and climb the hillside into Great Wood, following white arrows for a mile under the beech, yew and ash trees. 'No FP' ('no footpath') markings shepherd you away from side turnings. At the top edge of the trees (766901), aim half-right across a field for the corner of a wood, and cut across its neck to turn left at the road (765904). In 150 yards the road bends right; go left here (bridleway sign), keeping right where the path forks in 250 yards, to walk for a mile through the wood to meet a track. In 200 yards the trees end (757891) within sight of Kimble Farm; turn left here between posts (white arrows), bearing left in 50 yards at the top of a rise to find a stile at the upper edge of the woodland (758889). Cross the field to the road and walk forward (signed 'Fawley 1, Henley 5') for ¼ mile to turn left down the drive of Upper Woodend Farm (759883 – bridleway sign).

Fifty yards past a left-hand bend in the drive, turn right (blue bridleway sign) in a tunnel of trees, following white arrows into Great Wood and descending to a junction of tracks in a valley

(767877). Cross the junction and take the path opposite (double-headed white arrows; public footpath HA42 sign), and follow HA42 signs to a gateway at the edge of the wood (774873). Cross the field to a white arrow on a post, and in 25 yards turn right in the fringes of a wood to bear left along the track at the bottom; then right at the road for 250 yards and left over a stile (footpath sign) to cross a field and turn left again into Hambleden.

4

Henley, Hambleden Lock and Mill, and Aston
(Berks)

INFORMATION

Map OS 1:50,000 Landranger Sheet 175 'Reading and Windsor'.
Travel
>   TRAIN (BR) – Henley station.
>   CAR – M4 to Jct 9; A423 to Henley. Park at station, or by river south of bridge (free).
>   BUS – Green Line (Victoria) 081 668–7261. Local information: 0865 727000 (Oxford Tube bus company). London Victoria–Henley: bus stops in Hart Street, 200 yards from bridge.

Length of walk 6 miles – circular – start and finish at Henley station.
Conditions Well surfaced riverside path, field tracks, woodland paths.
Refreshments Flower Pot Hotel, Aston; many pubs and tea shops in Henley.
Reading
>   *Rambling for Pleasure Along the Thames* published by East Berks Ramblers Association Group – available from Pat Hayers, 16 Lanterns Walk, Farthingales, Maidenhead, Berks SL6 1TG.
>   *A Guide to the Thames Path* by Miles Jebb (Constable).

A walk of contrasts, from the bustling, colourful waterfront of Henley-on-Thames into quiet farming countryside caught in a great loop of the River Thames. From the setting for the world's most famous regatta the river leads you through broad meadows and past rich men's follies and mansions to an exciting catwalk over Hambleden's weirs. Then the atmosphere changes and you stroll among cornfields and woods, stopping at one of Berkshire's most appealing pubs on the way.

From Henley railway station (763823) walk down Station Road towards the river, bearing left into Thames-side which leads you to

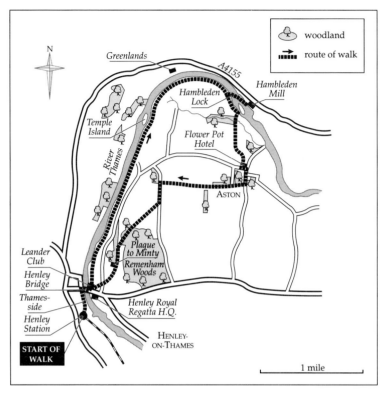

Henley Bridge (764826) beside the old, black-beamed and low-ceilinged Angel Inn. Cross the river from Oxfordshire into Berkshire.

On the far bank, upstream of the bridge, stands the florid modern headquarters of Henley Royal Regatta, while on the downstream side is the more modest clubhouse of the Leander Club, the pink-blazered social Mecca of Britain's discerning rowers. 'Henley Royal Regatta H.Q. has the power in the rowing world, but Leander has the fun', say locals. Fun is what Henley week, held in late June or early July, is all about – a social event to rank with Wimbledon or Cowes weeks, when straw boaters, blazers and champagne reassert their annual grip for the best part of a week on the small old town by the Thames. Flags flutter, bunting streams and the grandstands by the river are crammed with fine folk. It was all very different back in 1829 when Oxford and Cambridge Universities raced each other for the first time between Hambleden Lock and Henley Bridge. Cambridge wore pink colours and lost the race in front of a handful of onlookers. Ten years later four crews took part in the first official regatta, the whole event being over in three hours. But after Prince Albert became patron in 1851, the year of the Great Exhibition, the regatta became 'royal' and never looked back.

Just beyond the Berkshire end of the bridge turn left (green footpath sign) along the river bank.

From here you can admire the balconies, flower baskets and immaculate white paintwork of the riverside houses and pubs of Henley, the chequered flint-work tower of the church standing tall above their red-tiled roofs. Every house in Henley seems to be staring with all its windows at the river. The path runs at first past rowing club buildings and grandstands, then through more open meadows. Coots, moorhens, grebes, swans and gulls bob on the broad Thames as it runs north as a straight highway for over a mile, passing the cupola-crowned 18th-century folly designed by James Wyatt on the mid-river Temple Island, shaded by splendid willows, elders, birches and poplars (771847). This is where the regatta crews begin their race of 1 mile 550 yards to Henley Bridge. Beyond Temple Island the river makes a great loop from north to south, and here on the far bank you pass Greenlands, a white-faced Italianate wedding-cake of a mansion (775854), and shortly afterwards come to Hambleden lock and weirs (782851) and mill (784850).

Greenlands nowadays houses Henley Management College, but when it was built in 1871 for W.H. Smith, the self-made newsagent and stationery tycoon, it was one of the grandest private houses in one of the most extensive estates along the Thames. Those were the days when anyone rich and influential enough could build and develop what they liked where they chose. The Greenlands Estate, almost 4,000 acres of it, was given to the National Trust by its owner, the 3rd Viscount Hambleden, in 1944 to safeguard its landscape and buildings and protect them from development – a nice irony.

Hambleden Lock is one of the 45 operated by the National Rivers Authority along the Thames. Caleb Gould was its most famous keeper from 1777 to 1822, a man who attributed his good health (he lived to the age of 92) to his habitual supper of onion porridge. You can cross the lock gates and pass the neat flowerbeds and clipped hedges of the present lock keeper's house to walk above the rushing weirs on a 300-yard catwalk to Hambleden Mill, a handsome weatherboarded building crowned with a little square observatory tower and weather vane, built around 1600, which ground corn until 1958 – now it has been converted into smart flats.

Just beyond the lock a wide track leaves the river, passing through open cornfields to reach the quiet hamlet of Aston. Turn left where the track meets a road; the admirable Flower Pot Hotel is on the left at the T-junction (785842).

Clean, bright, its wood-panelled bars hung with crossed oars and stuffed pike, serving excellent beer brewed in Henley and good lunches, with a tree-shaded garden at the back, the Flower Pot is perfect. The brewery has 'plans' for it, the landlady told me – God forbid.

Walk up the lane from the pub, and in 200 yards turn right beyond Highway Cottage (784840 – footpath sign), over two fields to a lane (782840) which leads though rolling cornfields, the Thames hidden by the swell of the ground, a peaceful world away from the bustle of Henley. Turn left at the road (773840), and in 200 yards right over a stile by a big oak (773837 – green public footpath sign), making diagonally across a field to enter Remenham Woods (770835). The path passes banks of foxgloves and pink rosebay willowherb to leave the woods at a stile (white arrow) and traverse a hillside before bearing left along the upper edge of a grove of trees (767832), emerging at a stile and green footpath sign.

Set into the ground by the sign is a touching memorial plaque to a much-loved dog. The plaque is made of plastic, now cracked and weathered, destined to crumble away before long unless some kind person undertakes its restoration.

'To all who may walk this way. Please let this tribute stand in memory of Minty, a little dog with a big, big heart. He roamed these lovely fields and woods in happy freedom, waiting always at this place for his mistress. He gave, with all the love and affection he had to offer, eight years of absolute happiness to two elderly humans. Thank you, Minty, wherever you are. March 4th 1970.'

Cross the mini golf course beyond to a stile (footpath sign), and another in the bottom left-hand corner of the next field. Cross the road (766827), walk along the path towards the river for 50 yards, and go left through the gates behind the Leander Club to reach the road by Henley Bridge.

· 5 ·

Cookham and
Winter Hill
(Berks)

INFORMATION

Map OS 1:50,000 Landranger Sheet 175 'Reading and Windsor'.
Travel
  TRAIN (BR) – Cookham station.
  CAR – M25 to Jct 15; M4 to Jct 7; A4 to Maidenhead; A4094
    to Cookham; B4447 to Cookham Rise. Park at Cookham
    station.
  BUS – Green Line (Victoria) 081 668–7261. Local infor-
    mation: 0494 520941 (Wycombe Bus Company). London
    Victoria–Maidenhead–Cookham BR station.
Length of walk 7 miles – circular – start and finish at Cookham
  station (✄ *short cut* – 5 miles).
Conditions Lanes, woodland and field paths. Quarry Wood can
  be very muddy; Winter Hill is steep and slippery.
Opening times *Stanley Spencer Gallery, Cookham* Easter–
  October 10.30–5.30; November–Easter, 11–5 weekends and
  Bank Holidays.
Refreshments Bel and The Dragon, Cookham; The Old Swan-
  Uppers, Cookham Rise; Inn on the Green, Cookham Dean.
Reading Stanley Spencer Gallery has books and booklets.

This looping stretch of the River Thames is celebrated in the work of
the two men round whom this walk is based – the artist Sir Stanley
Spencer, who lived and worked in Cookham, and the writer Kenneth
Grahame who lived at Cookham Dean. Spencer's paintings were
founded on the buildings, landscape and personalities of Cookham;
while Grahame's children's classic *The Wind in the Willows* was set in
the river country near his home. Linking the two settings are footpaths
through some of the Thames's best scenery.

**From Cookham station (886850) turn left over the level crossing,
and immediately left again along High Road to pass a school on
your left. The next house, Clievden View, on the corner of Worster**

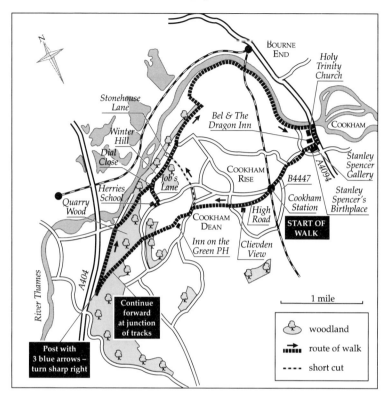

Road, was where Sir Stanley Spencer lived and painted from 1944 to the year of his death, 1959.

Spencer was knighted a few months before his death in recognition of his status as one of Britain's foremost artists. Instead of some grand house, he preferred to live in this modest, small brick villa in an unassuming village. We shall see one of his most accomplished paintings, *Christ Preaching at Cookham Regatta*, later in the walk – he painted it here in this house.

Continue up High Road to meet a road (880851), turn right for 50 yards, then left at a green footpath sign, skirting a playing field to turn right (footpath sign) and cross a shallow valley to the road at Cookham Dean (873853) (✂ *short cut* return route rejoins here) Follow the road to the left round an S-bend, and cut across the big green to the Inn on the Green pub. A footpath at the right side of the pub leads through trees, then right over a stile and across fields to a road in the valley (865853). Turn left, then immediately right (footpath sign) into Quarry Wood, a part of Bisham Woods.
    Follow blue bridleway arrows, keeping ahead at a junction of

tracks in 300 yards (860851) to descend a sunken lane which bends left and right and continues forward over another junction of tracks. In ¼ mile turn sharply back to the right (triangular post with 3 blue arrows), descending to walk along the bottom of the wood for ½ mile to reach a road (861857). Cross to a footpath (green sign) which climbs steeply up Winter Hill, then runs below a road to meet it at Dial Close near a popular viewpoint (870860).

Turn right here, then in 100 yards left down Job's Lane to a road.

Fifty yards up on your right is Herries prep school (868857). Here at the turn of the century, in this comfortable house with the Dutch gable and the verandah, lived Kenneth Grahame at the time he was writing *The Wind in the Willows*. Grahame made his name with the tale, written for his son Mouse. He had Winter Hill and Quarry Wood in mind when writing of the dreaded Wild Wood, and the stretch of the Thames between Marlow and Bourne End was the setting for the adventures of Rat, Mole, Toad and their friends and enemies. Returning to the viewpoint on Winter Hill, you can enjoy the whole 'Wind in the Willows' panorama.

Follow the road from the viewpoint, passing Stonehouse Lane on the left (✄ *short cut* – turn right up footpath opposite, to return to Cookham Dean). Take the next gravelled track to the left (875863 – National Trust 'Cock Marsh' sign), descending for ½ mile to the foot of the chalk ridge. Turn left here through a stile (882868) and follow green footpath signs to the river, which you follow for 1 ½ miles to the bridge at Cookham (898856). Climb up to the road and turn right for Holy Trinity Church; then follow the road round to the right into Cookham High Street.

A copy of Sir Stanley Spencer's *Last Supper* is in the church, along with some fine medieval brasses, but to enjoy the original painting visit the Stanley Spencer Gallery, on the left at the foot of the High Street (897853). Here a large collection of the artist's work is gathered – pencil drawings and paintings covering 50 years. There are exquisitely detailed paintings of trees, shrubs and houses, drawings of local children, and the big paintings of biblical themes by which he is best remembered. Spencer's subjects in these paintings are big, fleshy, vital people. The Apostles in the *Last Supper* have their large bare feet stuck well out from the table; while in the enormous, unfinished *Christ Preaching at Cookham Regatta*, Spencer's last work, Dionysian revellers sprawl on lawns and in punts around the central figure of Christ in a straw boater, bursting with energy as he leans forward to harangue his audience. Well-known local people are featured, including the landlord of the Ferry Inn and the boatman (with oars and paddles over his shoulder) who worked for Mr Turk the boatyard owner. Spencer adored

Cookham and its countryside, and the gallery's exhibition celebrates that life-long love.

Turn left out of the gallery up the High Street, passing on your left in 100 yards the house where Spencer was born in 1891 (blue plaque). Continue out of Cookham on the footpath beside the road into Cookham Rise, far less picturesque and dimity than Cookham, to reach the station.

·6·

Little Marlow, Hard-to-Find Farm and Horton Wood
(Bucks)

INFORMATION

Map OS 1:50,000 Landranger Sheet 175 'Reading & Windsor'.
Travel Car – M40 to Jct 4; A404; A4155. Park by Little
   Marlow church.
Length of walk 5 miles – circular – start and finish at Little
   Marlow church.
Conditions Woodland tracks; field paths; lanes.
Opening times St John the Baptist, Little Marlow – Sundays.
Refreshments Queen's Head or King's Head, Little Marlow.

This little slip of countryside is bounded by High Wycombe and the
M40 motorway on the north, the A404 dual carriageway on the west
and the Thames on the south – a green patch of woods and fields
hemmed in by the modern age. But Little Marlow, where the walk
begins, is a dream of a peaceful village, and the woods to the north
enfold you in the same tranquillity on this short but delightful walk.

A unique double lych-gate, operated by an ingenious pair of pulleys,
leads into the churchyard of St John the Baptist at Little Marlow
(874878). Light-coloured 15th-century roof timbers look down on the
barn-like aisles with their tall 14th- and 15th-century arches opening
into the nave. The chantry chapel at the east end of the south aisle contains a small but striking brass to Alice, wife of Sir Nicholas Ledewich,
who built the chapel (her lapdog with curled tail and ornate collar sits
alertly at her feet) and a snub-nosed angel in 15th-century stained glass,
his hair luxuriantly curly. There's also a fine plain Norman tub font and
many medieval windows.
   Little Marlow's 17th-century manor house stands just north of the
church, and flint-and-brick houses and garden walls line the village's
couple of streets, overhung with splendid old trees. There are two good
pubs, the Queen's Head down Pound Lane and the King's Head near
the A4155 road, and a cricket ground overlooked by a line of handsome, full-grown elms which have somehow escaped the devastation of

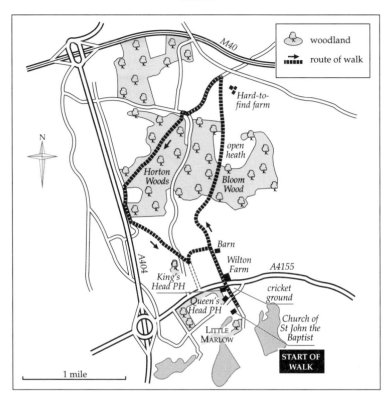

Dutch elm disease that has all but wiped out the elms of England in the last two decades. Little Marlow is a lovely village, undeveloped and complete.

From the church, walk up the lane to cross the A4155 (873881 – footpath sign) and continue through Wilton Farm's farmyard – note the timber framed, timber-clad and red-tiled old barn to your right. The farm track runs north in a wide, shallow valley of big fields gently billowing like plump yellow and green bolsters. One contains a black silhouette of a dog with cocked tail – to frighten the birds and rabbits, or to give them a good laugh?

The path bears left by an open-sided barn, and snakes on up to the corner of Bloom Wood (871892). Turn left here with the hedge on your right. In 100 yards, two tracks run into the wood to your right; take the second or lower one (white arrows on trees a little way into the wood), which descends to join a flinty track rising through a valley. In 200 yards leave it to the left (white arrows). In another 150 yards the path forks; go straight ahead with an iron gate on your right, and in another 250 yards join a green, grassy track diverging to the right (872897 – white arrow) to cross an

open heath among scrub of silver birch, dwarf oak, ash, sallow and alder. Soon you come to a crossing of tracks; keep ahead, following the left-hand curve of the track, to cross another track in a few yards and continue just inside the edge of the wood (white arrows), emerging from the trees (873902) to walk forward with a hedge on your right to reach the farm gate at Hard-to-Find Farm (873905).

Hard-to-Find Farm is not so lost and lonely as it used to be, with the M40 motorway rushing past just ahead. But it's still a wonderfully ramshackle and eccentric place, half flint-built and half weatherboarded, crowded with tall chimneys and oddly placed windows, roofs sloped at all angles, unexpected archways and corners. Nat Bowler, poet of Flackwell Heath, described Hard-to-Find Farm in the 1920s:

> 'So hard to find on yonder peak,
> This farmstead I desire to seek,
> Old oak beams and wooden shacks,
> Barley, rye twixt sodden stacks . . .
> I walk through gate, mid creepers climb,
> And all around was "Hard to Find".'

From the farm gate go left for 10 yards, then right over a stile to descend through a kissing gate into a lane (873908), where you turn left and go down to a junction of roads (869903). Turn right, and in 50 yards left (footpath sign) to walk through Horton Woods, following white arrows, for the best part of a mile.

The beech trees in Horton Wood grow 70 and 80 feet tall, filtering a tender, silvery-green light down to the bare floor of the wood, where undergrowth has failed to compete with the poisonous drip from the beech leaves. The M40 and A404 highways with their swishing traffic are less than a mile away, but only the faintest rumour of their roar reaches the depths of these dense, soothing woodlands.

One hundred yards past some pheasant-rearing pens the path bears left between the wood and a conifer plantation, dips to cross a hollow and continues to a lane beside the roaring A404 dual carriageway (860894). Turn left along this abandoned road and, just after the wood ends, left again over a stile (860889), to cross fields diagonally for half a mile down to a lane (876885). Cross here and climb the hillside opposite, to follow the farm track round a dog-leg before bending right to return to Wilton Farm, the A4155 and Little Marlow.

Burnham Beeches, Dorney Wood and Littleworth Common (Bucks)

INFORMATION

Map OS 1:50,000 Landranger Sheet 175 'Reading and Windsor'.
Travel CAR – M4 to Jct 6; A355 north
Length of walk 5 miles – circular – start and finish at car park on East Burnham Common.
Conditions Woodland tracks, field paths, short road stretches. Take tree book.
Opening times *Dorney Wood House* Grounds open by arrangement, August and September Saturdays 2.15–6.00. Write to the Secretary, Dorneywood Trust, Burnham Beeches, Bucks.
Refreshments Stag Inn, East Burnham Common; Blackwood Arms, Jolly Woodman or Beech Tree, Littleworth Common.
Reading *Rambling for Pleasure in East Berkshire* (green booklet), published by East Berks Ramblers' Association Group – available from Pat Hayers, 16 Lanterns Walk, Farthingales, Maidenhead, Berks SL6 1TG.

Burnham Beeches is an area deservedly popular with Londoners and Buckinghamshire people alike, so this is a walk best done out of the summer holiday season. Spring or autumn will show you these ancient beech woods at their best, preferably on a bright day when the sun slants through the leaves and lights up the grotesquely twisted trunks of Europe's oldest beech trees. A good pub and a famous political house are other features of the walk as it leaves the woods for the farmland around Dorney Wood.

From the big car park opposite the Stag Inn on East Burnham Common (956850), walk along the roadway into the trees, taking a fork to the right up Halse Drive (954850) 300 yards from the Stag Inn. Halse Drive drops into a hollow and climbs again, passing a turning on the right and continuing to a T-junction (946856)

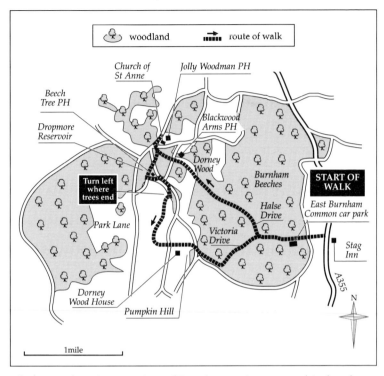

woodland — route of walk

Church of St Anne

Jolly Woodman PH

Beech Tree PH

Dropmore Reservoir

Blackwood Arms PH

Dorney Wood

Turn left where trees end

Burnham Beeches

START OF WALK

Halse Drive

East Burnham Common car park

Park Lane

Victoria Drive

Stag Inn

A355

N

Dorney Wood House

Pumpkin Hill

1mile

where stands a Corporation of London notice, covered in bye-laws, a strangely citified intrusion into these deep, quiet woodlands.

Much of the Chiltern landscape was still covered in beech woods in the 1870s, but they were beginning to disappear rapidly. One of many naturalists alarmed at this destruction, a Mr Heath, persuaded the City of London Corporation to buy the 600 acres of Burnham Beeches and dedicate them as a public open space. What the Corporation purchased in 1880 was the remnant of a great Saxon hunting forest, some of the trees themselves well over 300 years old. 'Most venerable beeches', the poet Gray had eulogised them, 'dreaming out their old stories to the winds'. Felix Mendelssohn had frequently got himself lost in these woods, maundering about on his visits to England in the 1830s and '40s. They were well known, but shamefully neglected, the smooth beech trunks grown fantastically gnarled and knotted, some hollow and splitting under the strain of supporting huge, overshot branches that should have been pollarded (following a custom four centuries old) for charcoal fuel – but charcoal had bowed to King Coal, and no one had trimmed the trees since the early years of the 19th century. Pollarding recommended after the purchase, and the beeches began to hold their own once more against nature's ever-vigilant invading armies of pine and silver birch.

These days all kinds of anti-development legislation safeguards Burnham Beeches. And the public still enjoys the freedom of the woods. You can follow paths just inside the trees beside Halse Drive, or plunge deeper in among the beeches where no car-borne visitors go (and very few walkers) to find wonderfully distorted old specimens. But take care. You might just sit down in the soothing silence and green half-light, and decide to stay put there for ever.

Cross over the T-junction on to the woodland path ahead. Soon you cross Park Lane (944856) into Dorney Wood. The footpath signs point both ways, but once over the stile bear diagonally right onto a path under silver birch and oak, which leads to a kissing gate (941859 – yellow arrow). Cross a field and a pair of stiles, then another pair, to reach a road by the Blackwood Arms (936863), a cosy pub with a variety of unusual beers. Cross the road and continue through the woodland of Littleworth Common to emerge on the road opposite the neat Victorian Church of St Anne (934864), built to serve the Dropmore Estate that was created out of scrubland in the 18th century by Lord Grenville. A gate in the northeast corner of the churchyard leads to a road; 10 yards to the right is the breezy and corporately smartened Jolly Woodman pub.

Back at St Anne's church, retrace your steps into the woods for 50 yards to a junction of tracks; turn to the right on a well-beaten path which crosses a road (934862) and snakes among the trees, passing to the left of Dropmore Reservoir to bear right at a house and meet a road on a sharp bend (933860). Turn left for 100 yards to the Beech Tree pub at a crossroads. Turn right along the road ('Burnham Beeches 2' sign), and in 50 yards go right over a stile (footpath sign), then left around a field edge which swings right to where the trees on your left come to an end (936857). Turn left here and walk south down three field edges, keeping the hedge on your left, to cross a stile at the bottom of the third field (934850); then turn left and follow the path diagonally across a field, aiming for a gap in the trees plugged by a stile and tall green pole and a footpath sign, where you meet a road (937850). In 100 yards to the right are the entrance gates to Dorney Wood House.

Dorney Wood House, a handsome red brick building, was given to the nation in 1942 by its owner, Lord Courtauld-Thomson, as a country retreat for Cabinet ministers. The Prime Minister has the unenviable task of deciding who shall enjoy Dorney Wood – Home Secretaries, Chancellors of the Exchequer and Foreign Secretaries have all been thus privileged. Eminent teeth have been sucked and famous feet stamped when Dorney Wood has been passed on to other temporary holders. It is a very desirable residence. The grounds are open to the public by appointment only (see information box above).

Back at the road crossing, continue over the stile opposite and along a field edge to reach the road on Pumpkin Hill (941850). Pass to the left of a big Corporation of London 'Burnham Beeches West' signboard and carry on along a green, grassy ride which drops downhill with a road close by on the right. At the bottom, turn left on to Victoria Drive (944846) and follow it for ⅓ mile to reach Halse Drive (950850), where you turn right to reach East Burnham Common and the car park.

· 8 ·

Hedgerley
and Stoke Common
(Bucks)

INFORMATION

Map OS 1:50,000 Landranger Sheet 176 'West London'.
Travel
  CAR – M40 to Jct 2; A355 towards Slough; Hedgerley road is
    on left, 2 miles from M40. Park by White Horse pub.
  BUS – Green Line (Victoria) 081 668–7261. Local informa-
    tion: 0296 382000. London Victoria–Slough–Hedgerley
    Hill: bus stops at top of Hedgerley Hill, ½ mile south of
    Hedgerley.
Length of walk 4½ miles – circular – start and finish at
  Hedgerley church.
Conditions Field and woodland paths (can be muddy); well
  surfaced bridleway across Stoke Common; short stretch of
  road.
Refreshments White Horse or Brickmould, Hedgerley.

Just how Hedgerley has managed to cling on to so much of its village atmosphere, so close to the M40 motorway and the conurbations of Gerards Cross and Slough, is known only to its inhabitants and the Lord. The woodland paths and the wide heath of Stoke Common are equally untainted by noise and rush. This is a short walk to savour.

Hedgerley's medieval trade in the making of pottery and roof tiles is echoed in the name of one of its pubs – the Brickmould. The other pub, the White Horse, stands only a couple of hundred yards up the village street, with all of Hedgerley lined up in between – the 'Buckinghamshire Best Kept Village' sign opposite the stately three-storied red brick Court Farm, the long Dean Cottages with their curious triangular bay windows facing the murky village pond, and the solid old house and half-timbered barn of Metcalfe Farm a little higher up the street.
  Below the White Horse pub, a path leads up to the right to reach flint-built St Mary's Church on its knoll, a Victorian rebuilding

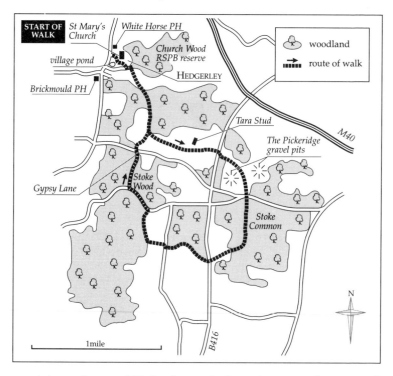

containing a decorated Tudor font, a lively 17th-century depiction of what happens to sinners who break the Ten Commandments and a 17th-century satinwood pulpit brought from a church in Antigua.

From the church (971873), go through the kissing gate in the south-east corner of the churchyard, cross a field to a stile and turn left along the lane to a stile by a gate (972872). The RSPB's Church Wood reserve is on your left, with trails and a hut with a book recording sightings. From the gate bear right diagonally across the field (footpath sign), making for a stile at the edge of the wood (974870). The path rises through the trees, knobbled with roots, to emerge at the top along a grassy path to a plank footbridge and stile among trees at the end of the field (975864). Turn left here to cross fields and reach a stile into a lane opposite Tara Stud Farm (979862).

At Tara Stud they breed Welsh ponies for showing, buying the brood mares from the sales at Hereford and hoping to get perhaps two potential winners from every 15 foals. The little Class A mountain ponies used to be bred for work in the coal pits – small and stocky, their pretty faces show the influence of an Arab stallion that once roamed the Welsh hills. Bigger ponies, Class C and D, go between the shafts of gigs as 'driving ponies'.

Take the path to the right of Tara Stud, over a gate in 100 yards and on with a hedge on your left to cross the B416 by stiles (983862 – footpath sign). The signs lead you through the middle of The Pickeridge Farm – no longer a farm, but a mass of huge holes from which dinosaur-necked dredgers scoop out thousands of tons of gravel and sand. **Walk up the concrete drive to the road (987857), and turn a few yards to the right to cross onto a bridle-way (white horseshoe sign) which runs due south across the wide open spaces of Stoke Common.**

Here is a place where no gravel dredgers have come – no developers, no road builders, no golf course designers. Stoke Common stretches as far as you can see, a flat, boggy heath thick with scrub trees – silver birch, dwarf oak, willow, sallow. Star-like green mosses grow here, along with common heather and bell heather, bracken and sedge. Tall, dark pines stand in clumps among the scrub. It's a sombre, windy, lonely place, a precious remnant of the heathland that once blanketed the country south-west of London. Man simply doesn't signify here.

The gravelly bridleway runs south across the common to enter the woods and meet an ancient boundary bank. Turn right here, and in 300 yards right again, to meet the B416 in ¼ mile (982849). I'm still not sure why the path appears to make three sides of a square while turning a simple right-angle on the map!

Cross the road onto a path (footpath sign; 'Beeches Way' way-mark), and in a few yards bear right, following 'Beeches Way' signs across more open common land, to bear left (blue 'Beeches Way' waymark) through a silver birch copse, across a path (yellow 'Beeches Way' sign) to meet a road (977851). Cross the road over a stile, and pass a line of old hollies to a stile into woodland (974851). A blue 'Beeches Way' sign points left, but turn right inside the edge of the wood, then left along a road (974855). Take the first lane on the right, Gypsy Lane, which snakes under the beeches of Stoke Wood to a road (973862). Turn left and in 20 yards a green footpath sign across the road points over a field to the corner of a wood, where at the stile you meet the path down which you retrace your steps to Hedgerley.

9

Bayhurst Wood, Mad Bess Wood
and Ruislip Lido
(Middlesex)

INFORMATION

Map OS 1:50,000 Landranger Sheet 176 'West London'.
Travel
  TUBE – West Ruislip (Central line).
  CAR – M25 to Jct 16; M40 towards London for 2½ miles;
    B467 to Ickenham; left on B466. Park near West Ruislip
    tube station (⅔ mile).
Length of walk 6½ miles – circular – start and finish at West
  Ruislip tube station (✂ *short cut* – 5 miles).
Conditions Field and woodland paths, which can be very boggy
  after rain.
Opening times Ruislip Lido 10–8 (summer); 8–4 (winter).
Refreshments The Soldier's Return (near West Ruislip tube
  station).
Reading Leaflets on Bayhurst, Mad Bess and Copse Woods, and
  on the northern section of the Hillingdon Trail (Ruislip Lido
  to Ickenham Green) available from Leisure Services
  Department, London Borough of Hillingdon (0895 250111).

Three long-established woods, each with its own special character, each
well provided with paths; an early 19th-century canal reservoir turned
into a water-sporting lake; centuries-old green lanes; wide views over
wooded farmland. These are the pleasures of this country walk from
the western suburbs of London.

**From West Ruislip station (084868) turn left along the B466, then
right just beyond the Soldier's Return pub (081865) on to a path
which crosses a ditch in 200 yards. Follow the left bank of the ditch
for ½ mile to go under a railway line (073871) and turn left to cross
a road by Gates Mead Farm into an old lane (073873 – bridleway
sign).**

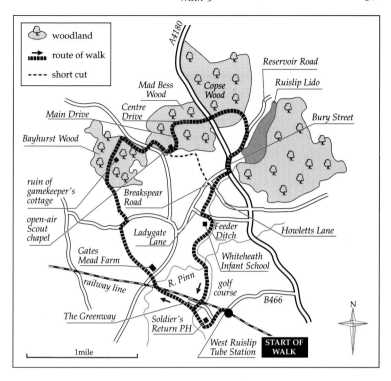

This lane has nothing to do with London or its suburbia, and everything to do with the countryside. Its tall hedges, 15 feet thick, grow oak, elder, hawthorn, blackthorn, beech and field maple – they may be six or seven hundred years old. From the crest of the lane, wide views open out over the wooded expanses of West Middlesex and Hertfordshire.

At the road (068880) turn right for 100 yards, then left over a stile (yellow arrow and footpath sign) to walk over the fields up to Bayhurst Wood. The horse riders' boggy morass of a bridleway is separated from the walkers' drier footpath here by a fence – an excellent idea for both.

   At the stile into Bayhurst Wood (066886), bear diagonally left up through the trees for 100 yards to find a wild service tree beside a junction of paths – a rare tree, and a good indicator of ancient woodland, with toothed leaves deeply cut into nine or 10 'fingers'. Back at the wood entrance, walk forward for 50 yards to turn right opposite a pond and climb a path through the wood (post with 'No Horses' sign).

On each side are old coppiced hornbeams, uncut for generations, their long, smooth grey branches shooting up towards the canopy of the wood. At the top of the rise a pile of bricks under leaf-mould on your right marks the site of a gamekeeper's cottage – what a splendidly peaceful and isolated place to live, with only the squirrels, pheasants and jays for company.

Descend to turn right (068893) inside the wood's edge to meet a lane (071890); turn left to cross a road and turn right inside the southern edge of Mad Bess Wood. In 250 yards bear left at a triangular footpath sign (074890) (✄ *short cut* – keep ahead here to turn right in ¼ mile and rejoin walk in Howlett's Lane). Walk north for 200 yards to another triangular sign (077892).

The square-clipped hedge of beech and hornbeam on your left here encloses a grassy rectangle with a cross inlaid in crazy-paving on its floor. This is an open-air chapel dedicated by the Scout movement to the young men of Ruislip who died in the Second World War.

Bear left here and walk up Main Drive, another old green lane, wide, straight and well surfaced – a lane with the air of going somewhere purposefully.

In 200 yards turn right along Centre Drive (075894; footpath sign) to cross the A4180 into Copse Wood (082895; footpath sign). In 250 yards reach a wooden post marked with a white arrow pointing forward; bear right downhill here, forking right as you leave the trees onto the path beside Ruislip Lido (087894).

You can walk a circuit of this big stretch of water, ride round most of it on a miniature train, swim or fish, water ski or just loaf about. The Lido started life as a reservoir, created by damming the stream in 1804 to feed the newly opened Grand Junction Canal to Paddington. Soon the railways had taken most of the canal's business, and the lake became a popular place for a day out, as it is today.

Walk down Reservoir Road to turn left along A4180 Bury Street for 100 yards. In the angle of Breakspear Road and Bury Street (084888) a footpath sign points across fields beside the meandering Cannonbrook, to cross Howletts Lane (✄ *short cut* – rejoins) and join a road through housing. Turn left on Ladygate Lane (081882), then right beside Whiteheath Infant School (footpath sign). In 200 yards the path forks; bear left by a fence along the top of a field to cross the River Pinn (081875).

The elegantly curved little bridge also carries a concrete trough in which once flowed the Feeder Ditch, taking water from Ruislip Lido to the canal at Southall. But the feeder was too long, its slope too shallow. It silted up, and 50 years after the reservoir was built it had become redundant.

Cross the next field and a plank footbridge, go through a belt of trees and keep the same line southwards across the fairways of a golf course, with the Feeder Ditch (sometimes underground) always on your left. In ⅓ mile the path goes under the railway (080870) and crosses The Greenway road, continuing for 150 yards to the bridge over the Feeder Ditch (080867) where you turn left for the Soldier's Return and West Ruislip station.

10

Horsenden Hill,
Perivale
(Middlesex)

INFORMATION

Map
> OS 1:50,000 Landranger Sheet 176 'West London'.
> Excellent large-scale map in Ealing Borough Council's
> *Horsenden Hill Countryside Walk* guide booklet
> (tel: 081 579–2424).
> More general map – pages 39 and 40 of the *London A–Z*.

Travel
> TUBE – Perivale (Central line)
> CAR – A40 west out of central London to Hanger Lane
> roundabout; right along A4005 (Hanger Lane becomes
> Ealing Road, then Bridgewater Road); left along A4090
> Whitton Avenue East; left down Melville Avenue, which
> becomes Horsenden Lane North. Park at Ballot Box pub,
> on left in ¼ mile.
> BUS – 071 222–1234 (London Transport). Piccadilly line
> tube to Sudbury Town; H17 bus stops at Melville Avenue,
> 300 yards north of Ballot Box pub.

Length of walk
> If travelling by car: 2 miles – circular – start and finish at
> Ballot Box pub, Horsenden Lane North.
> If travelling by tube: 3½ miles – circular – start and finish at
> Perivale tube station

Conditions Woodland and field tracks. Some can be sticky
underfoot.

Selborne Society and Perivale Wood The Selborne Society of
naturalists looks after Perivale Wood, a remnant of a
medieval deer-hunting reserve still coppiced and carefully
maintained, crammed with wildlife of all sorts, that lies across
the Grand Union Canal from Horsenden Hill. You can enjoy
the freedom of Perivale Wood by joining the Selborne Society
before your walk (tel: 081 578–3181). The key to Perivale
Wood is held at Perivale Library (see below).

Opening times **Perivale Library** (on the corner of Horsenden
Lane South and Buckingham Avenue – *London A–Z* page 56
square A1) Tuesdays and Fridays 9–7.45; Thursdays and
Saturdays 9–5 (tel: 081 997–2830).
Refreshments **Ballot Box pub, Horsenden Lane North.**
Reading
Horsenden Hill Countryside Walk booklet (see above).
A Farm in Perivale by Eva Farley, and *The Chronicles of
Greenford Parva* by J. Allen Brown – both available at
Perivale Library.

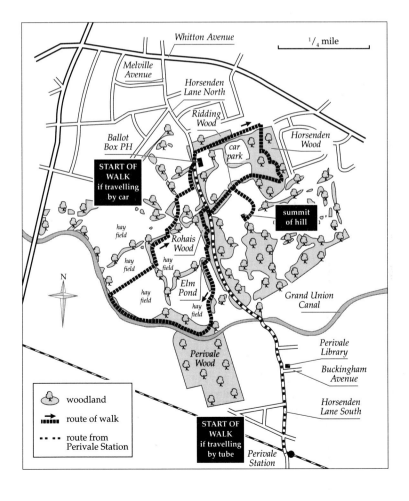

This is a country walk in character rather than in geographical fact; Perivale lies mid-way between Wembley and Ealing in suburban west London. But Horsenden Hill, raising its 250 acres of flowery grassland and woods above the surrounding houses, owes nothing to London for its atmosphere. Here an ancient rural landscape has been preserved, a green oasis of peaceful countryside looked after in traditional ways that have stood the test of the centuries. To walk on Horsenden Hill is to take a stroll back through time, in a little corner of old-fashioned rural England, miraculously surviving in one of the world's great cities.

The large and popular Ballot Box pub is named after an earlier pub that stood nearer the canal where, at general elections in Victorian times, the bargemen would cast their votes while having a drink.

The Ballot Box pub is the starting point for this walk. To reach it from Perivale tube station (164833), turn right and walk up Horsenden Lane past Perivale Library, to cross the Grand Union Canal (162839) and carry on beside Horsenden Lane on a path among trees to the right, up and over Horsenden Hill to find the Ballot Box on your right at the foot of the hill (159847).
    From The Ballot Box turn right down the lane, and immediately right again along a surfaced path inside the edge of Ridding Wood for ¼ mile, to turn right uphill at the far corner (162848) into Horsenden Wood.

Note the wild service tree with pointed, toothed, finger-like leaves beside Post 19, a sure indicator of long-established woodland. The path through Horsenden Wood climbs among twisted old hornbeams with smooth grey trunks, which, along with oak and hazel, were coppiced here for centuries. This is a beautifully quiet stretch of ancient wood.

Bear right just before the trees end on a track which leads to a car park (161846); turn left here to climb to the 276-foot summit of Horsenden Hill.

From this open dome of grass you can see (on a clear day) six counties and 10 London boroughs. The view is immense, from Surrey, Middlesex, Buckinghamshire and Berkshire over to the great eastward sprawl of London, with the dome of St Paul's Cathedral pricking the skyline 10 miles away.

Return to the car park, bearing right across the road entrance for a few yards to cross Horsenden Lane (160845) and turn left through Rohais Wood.

The path winds between wildly overgrown hedges of privet, laurel and Japanese bamboo, past flights of steps leading nowhere and fragments of rockery wall. This now tangled strip of woodland was the garden of Rohais House, pulled down in the 1940s. Piles of cut timber have been left on the ground to rot, so that insects can feed on the dead wood.

Shortly after the path leaves the trees you pass Elm Pond, where elm suckers, regenerating after the country-wide ravages of Dutch elm disease, have been laid in a plaited hedge.

The big fields to your right are cut in summer for hay, to allow traditional meadow flowers such as ragged robin, buttercups and bird's-foot trefoil to set seed and grow, making the fields a marvellous sight in summer. Before the big factories moved out here along the Great West Road in the 1930s, Perivale was a small farming community producing hay for the army and for London's huge number of working horses.

Continue south along the path to turn right beside the Grand Union Canal (159839) for ¼ mile.

The canal (known then as the Grand Junction Canal) reached Perivale in 1801. Barges carried hay up to London and brought back horse manure for the fields, as well as loads of the city's rubbish which was tipped in Perivale Wood just across the water. In spring the wood is hazed with bluebells, one among many plant species that thrive in this expertly managed nature reserve.

At Post 14, by a cast-iron canal company boundary marker (155840), turn right on a path that leads across the hay fields for ⅔ mile, past hedges cut and laid in traditional fashion, to return to the Ballot Box.

Horsenden Hill rises to your right, a thickly-wooded dome. If dusk has fallen and it's a moonlit evening you may hear the hooves of Horsa's steed clopping inside the hill. Legend says that Horsa, a Saxon warlord, killed while avenging the wrongs done to his beautiful daughter Ealine by her drunken brute of a husband, lies buried with his warhorse in Horsenden Hill.

All the richness of wildlife and natural beauty of this little Garden of Eden in west London, so sensitively maintained by Ealing Borough Council, would have been lost for ever under the building developments of the 1930s if Middlesex County Council had not had the great good sense to buy up Horsenden Hill as a public open space. Raise a glass to its foresight as you relax in the Ballot Box after your walk.

Amersham
and Chalfont St Giles
(Bucks)

INFORMATION

Map OS 1:50,000 Landranger Sheet 176 'West London'.
Travel

TUBE – Amersham (Metropolitan line).

CAR – M25 to Jct 18, A404 to Amersham-on-the-Hill. Park at tube station.

BUS – Green Line (Victoria) 081 668–7261. Local information: 0296 382000. London Victoria–Beaconsfield (Old Hare) –Amersham station.

Length of walk 8 miles – circular – start and finish at Amersham tube station (✂ *short cut* – 6½ miles).

Conditions Field and woodland paths – stretches can be muddy.

Refreshments Several pubs and hotels in Amersham; Fox and Hounds, Chalfont St Giles.

Reading Booklets on John Milton from Milton's Cottage, Chalfont St Giles.

Amersham's atmospheric old town stands at one end of the walk; Chalfont St Giles at the other, with memories of one of England's greatest poets. In between runs the River Misbourne, which may not be there at all! And in the midst of typically beautiful Chiltern countryside there's a painful reminder of religious intolerance that saw dissenters burned in Tudor Amersham.

From Amersham tube station (963982) turn left under two bridges and immediately right (footpath sign) along a pathway. Bear left before reaching a road (961982), keeping to the path along the top edge of Parsonage Woods, then descending the hill to reach St Mary's Church (958974) in Old Amersham.

The exterior of St Mary's Church bulges characterfully with flint-built chapels, but the interior is disappointingly over-restored with Victorian zeal. The old High Street is a nice place to wander, though, lined with

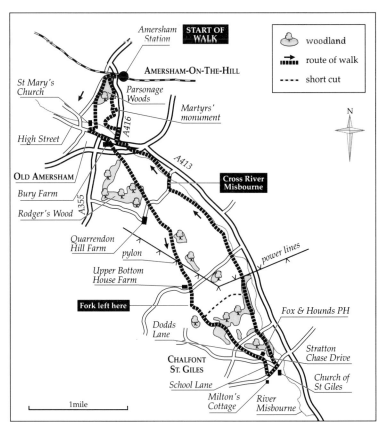

17th- and 18th-century red brick houses and inns, all centred on the big brick market hall of 1682. Amersham-on-the-Hill grew up round the Metropolitan tube station at the turn of the 20th century, leaving the old town unspoiled in the valley below.

From St Mary's Church turn left along the High Street, continuing forward where the A355 goes off to the right. In 50 yards turn right (South Bucks Way sign) through the farmyard of Bury Farm, under the A413 and up and away for two glorious miles, following yellow arrow waymarks. Aim high to cut across the corner of Rodger's Wood (968964) and keep a straight line across fields to the right-hand corner of a copse (973956), enjoying superb views over the Misbourne valley, gently rolling and crowned with trees.

From the copse bear diagonally right to a pylon, make for a stile in the hedge ahead and descend a slope to Upper Bottom House Farm in the depths of a quiet valley. Turn right at the road (976947), and in 20 yards left (footpath sign) up an old track,

forking left (976944) and keeping straight ahead where the track swings left, to reach a lane at the top of the hill (979943) (✄ *short cut* – bear left in front of Hill Farm House). In 200 yards bear left at a fork and walk down to a crossroads (983939); cross into Dodds Lane, and opposite the Fox and Hounds (989935) bear right along School Lane to reach a road in Chalfont St Giles just below Milton's cottage (989933).

John Milton came to his 'Pretty Box at Giles Chalfont' in 1665, in flight from the plague ravaging London. The blind poet was not too popular at the time, owing to his steadfast support of Oliver Cromwell throughout the 11 years of the Commonwealth. With King Charles II now restored to the throne, Milton lay low at Chalfont St Giles for a year, finishing his epic poem *Paradise Lost* and starting its sequel, *Paradise Regained.*

The poky little brick-and-timber cottage has altered hardly at all since Milton's residence, though there are stairs to the upper floor today – the poet himself, unable to see, probably did not risk the ladder that was the only way of gaining the upstairs region of the cottage at that time. There's a good Milton exhibition in the museum – rare editions, letters, personal possessions and a lock of his hair.

Down the hill the church of St Giles contains wonderfully preserved 14th-century wall paintings – Creation with a joyfully leaping lion and leopard, Adam and Eve getting their marching orders from an angel, the Crucifixion, Salome with the head of John the Baptist – and some interesting monuments, including the one to the prolific Sir Thomas Fleetwoode, who fathered 18 children.

Just below the Crown Inn turn left up Stratton Chase Drive (990935) and walk 2½ miles up the Misbourne valley, following South Bucks Way signs and yellow arrows (✄ *short cut* – rejoins here.). At the track from Quarrendon Hill Farm turn right (972963) to cross the River Misbourne; turn left along its bank and continue under the A413 (966969) to a roundabout (963971).

The Misbourne is a 'winterbourne', a river that disappears from time to time. Abnormally dry seasons may be responsible, or excessive pumping, or cracks in its bed, or – according to local legend – the threat of war. In 1914 it vanished, and again in 1939.

Turn right uphill at the roundabout, then in 70 yards left (footpath sign), dog-legging up the hillside to the right to find the Amersham martyrs' monument (963975).

Amersham was a great centre for religious dissent in Tudor times, and some of the Protestant dissenters paid for their freedom of conscience with their lives. They were burned at a spot near the monument –

William Tylsworth in 1506, six others in 1521. Tylsworth and one of the later martyrs, John Scrivener, had their pyres lit by their own children under coercion. Less than 20 years later, King Henry VIII ventured down the Protestant path himself, and then the boot of intolerance was forced firmly onto the other foot.

Continue up the field edge and through the neck of Parsonage Wood to rejoin the path back to Amersham tube station.

12

Little Chalfont to Latimer, Church End and Chenies
(Bucks)

INFORMATION

Map OS 1:50,000 Landranger Sheet 176 'West London'.
Travel
    TUBE – Chalfont & Latimer (Metropolitan line).
    CAR – M25 to Jct 18; A404 to Little Chalfont. Car park at
      tube station.
Length of walk 7 miles – circular – start and finish at Chalfont
    & Latimer tube station (✂ *short cut* – 3½ miles).
Conditions Woodland and riverside paths; field paths; farm
    tracks. Sections can be muddy, especially in woods above
    Little Chalfont.
Opening times Chenies House April–October, Wednesdays and
    Thursdays 2–5.
Refreshments Cock Inn, Church End.
Reading *Discovering Walks in the Chilterns* by Ron Pigram
    (Shire Publications). Church notes at Holy Cross, Church
    End; St Michael's, Chenies.

Arriving at Little Chalfont by tube, you find yourself in a few minutes exploring the beautiful valley of the River Chess – Latimer village, as pretty as a picture round its green; Latimer House tall and imposing in red brick; a stroll past a lonely tomb in the meadows to a tiny medieval church with wall paintings 600 years old. More riverside ramblings bring you back to the tube station by way of one of England's finest Tudor houses, and probably the best collection of memorial tombs anywhere in the country.

From Chalfont & Latimer tube station (997975) walk down the approach road and turn sharp left along Bedford Avenue, then right in 250 yards up Chenies Avenue (996976). Cross Elizabeth Avenue and continue forward to where Chenies Avenue bends left into Beechwood Avenue (996981). Walk ahead here down a gravelly path and bear right into the woods, then left in 10 yards

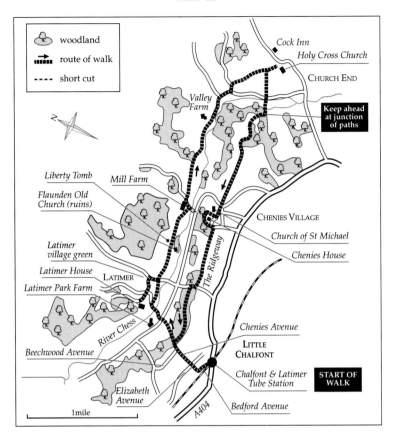

woodland

route of walk

---- short cut

Cock Inn

Holy Cross Church

CHURCH END

Valley Farm

Keep ahead at junction of paths

Liberty Tomb

Mill Farm

Flaunden Old Church (ruins)

CHENIES VILLAGE

Church of St Michael

Chenies House

Latimer village green

Latimer House

LATIMER

Latimer Park Farm

The Ridgeway

River Chess

Beechwood Avenue

Chenies Avenue

LITTLE CHALFONT

Chalfont & Latimer Tube Station

START OF WALK

Elizabeth Avenue

Bedford Avenue

A404

1 mile

downhill to cross a lower path and continue down to the edge of the wood. Walk down across fields, with a view ahead over Latimer Park Farm to the multiple chimneys and gables of Latimer House dominating the slope opposite. Cross the road (999985) and the field beyond, then the bridge over the River Chess, stopping here to enjoy this delectable stretch of peaceful English countryside where great horse chestnuts, silver birch and plane trees stand along the river which flows down its quiet valley through beds of watercress – an ordered, landscaped slice of rural heaven. Then turn right over a stile and walk beside the river to a road (003988), where you turn left to reach Latimer village green.

Charming old brick-and-timber cottages surround the little triangular green, where three items catch the eye – the village pump under a tiled pagoda roof, the obelisk memorial to local men who served in the Boer War, and the cairn commemorating Villebois, the favourite horse of the French General de Villebois Mareuil who was killed at the Battle of

Boshof on 5th April 1900, in the act of saving the life of Charles Compton Cavendish, Lord Chesham of Latimer. The grateful Lord Chesham had Villebois (the horse) brought back to England to end his days at Latimer, and when he died in 1911 the nobleman caused his heart to be buried here on the green along with his harness and ceremonial trappings.

Lord Chesham's red brick mansion, Latimer House, stands just up the road (000989). Built for the Cavendish family in 1863, it saw service recently as the National Defence College for NATO officers before entering on its present role as a conference centre and training college for accountants.

Retrace your steps from the village green for 50 yards; then turn left over a stile (Chess Valley Walk sign) and follow a path through the fields which soon passes above a tangled copse hiding the remnants of Flaunden Old Church (009987).

The few remnants of the flint walls of the medieval church are smothered in bushes and nettles at the nearest corner of the trees. It was left to fall down when a new church was built a mile to the north on higher ground. But the old church was anathema in its operative days to at least one freethinking local craftsman. Just above the ruins of the church you pass the modest, brick-built tomb under two oaks where 'Mr William Liberty of Chorleywood, Brickmaker' lies buried with his wife Alice. Mr Liberty – what more appropriate surname could he have had? – died in 1777, having stipulated that he should not be laid to rest anywhere within the bounds of the church.

Continue ahead, following blue leaping trout waymarks, to cross the farmyard of Mill Farm (014988) – note the old wooden pigeon loft and the weather-vane with a cow on top (✂ *short cut* – turn right here across T-junction, on footpath to Church of St Michael at Chenies.). Turn left up the road for 100 yards, then right over a stile (Chess Valley Walk sign) to walk through meadows and woodland to the road below Valley Farm (026990). Keep straight ahead down a lane to turn right along a road (031990); follow round a left-hand bend, then in 100 yards turn right over a stile (033990). The sign here says 'Church End 1½' – in fact it's not much more than half a mile across the fields to Holy Cross Church (039984).

The stubby little flint 12th-century church, with its tower capped with Tudor brick and a steeply pitched saddle-back roof, stands a mile south of its parent village of Sarratt, with a cool and beautiful interior where arches of many architectural eras stand under dark medieval roof timbers. On the east wall of the south transept are paintings dating from the 1370s, showing a slim Virgin with hands raised as Gabriel announces the advent of Christ, a shepherd hurrying to Bethlehem clutching a lamb as an angel blows a double-piped shawm, and a sea of faces below, looking up over a forest of piously folded hands.

Leave the church through the south gate in the churchyard, opposite the brick almshouses of 1821 (the Cock Inn is just up the road to the left), and turn right over a stile to reach the valley bottom (035981), where you turn right across a field to the next stile (033984). Turn left here to cross the River Chess and a second (sometimes dry) stream to reach a junction of paths (032984). Go forward over two stiles (yellow and white arrows), across fields and along the edge of a wood, to join a farm track (025984) which brings you to Chenies village.

This model estate village was built in the 1850s by the Duke of Bedford, owner of the great Tudor manor house of Chenies that sits among its trees at the western edge of the village (014984). The many tall chimney stacks on the cottages echo those on the master house, owned by the Russell family, Dukes of Bedford, from 1526 until 1954 when it was sold to pay death duties. Before the 17th century, when the Russells moved to Woburn Abbey and Chenies became ruinous, the great house had played host to England's great and good. In 1534 the lame King Henry VIII is reputed to have spent the night wandering the corridors in search of his wife Katharine Howard, who was carrying on an affair. His ghost still walks Chenies, dragging a lame leg.

With its crow-stepped gables and intricately twisted tall chimneys, Chenies looms massively over the 15th-century Church of St Michael, gloomy inside under its heavy Victorian roof, whose entire north side was converted in 1556 into the Bedford Chapel and filled in the following four centuries with the grandest of Russell monuments – among them are John Russell, the 1st Earl (1486–1555); a languidly lounging figure of the 1st Duke of Bedford (1613–1700); Lord John Russell, the Victorian statesman and twice Prime Minister; the 'Flying Duchess', wife of the 12th Earl, who disappeared on a flight from Woburn in 1947 aged 80 and stone deaf. What a pity that the chapel is not open to the public, and can only be enjoyed through window glass.

Turn right between church and house (✂ *short cut* – rejoins here) to enter woodland, bearing left just inside (three-headed arrow on tree) and in 150 yards left again, following white arrows to emerge behind Chenies by a farm gateway (013984), through which you turn right along the stony track called The Ridgeway to reach a road (005982). Turn right, then in 50 yards go left (footpath sign) through woodland for ½ mile to reach the top of Chenies Avenue (996981) and drop down to the tube station.

13

Hemel Hempstead
and the Grand Union Canal,
Bourne End and Bovingdon
(Herts)

INFORMATION

Map OS 1:50,000 Landranger Sheet 166 'Luton and Hertford'.
Travel
  TRAIN (BR) – Hemel Hempstead.
  CAR – Ml to Jct 8; A414; A41. Car park next to station.
  BUS – Green Line (Victoria) 081 668–7261. Local
    information: 0923 257405. London Victoria–Hemel
    Hempstead bus station – numerous local buses to
    Hemel Hempstead BR station.
Length of walk 6 miles – circular – start and finish at Hemel
  Hempstead station.
Conditions Canal towpath; grassy footpaths; field paths. Two
  short stretches of road (pavements).
Refreshments Fishery Inn by canal, opposite Hemel Hempstead
  station; Three Horseshoes, Bourne End; Bobsleigh Inn on the
  B4505 north of Bovingdon.
Reading *Walk Herts and Bucks* by David Perrott and Laurence
  Main (Bartholomew Map and Guide).

These six miles in the open countryside south-west of Hemel
Hempstead railway station take you by way of the Grand Union Canal
– and memories of a terrible railway accident in the days of steam – to
a pretty old canal-side pub; then south into a quiet landscape of big
cornfields and woodland paths, before returning to the station between
two high and ancient commons rich in wildlife.

**From the station forecourt (043059), cross the A41 Berkhamsted
road and take the path opposite to the bridge and lock on the
Grand Union Canal by the Fishery Inn (043061). Turn left with-
out crossing the bridge and walk along the towpath through**

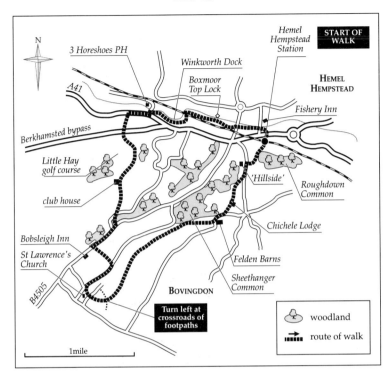

the valley of the River Bulbourne towards Bourne End, passing Boxmoor Top Lock with its lock-keeper's cottage (036062).

The Grand Union Canal began life as the Grand Junction Canal (note the mileage notice by the lock cottage gate), built on the initiative of the third Duke of Bridgewater between 1793 and 1806 to link up London and the Midlands. During construction in the Bulbourne Valley the navvies camped out in tents on Sheethanger Common, across the valley to your left, and terrified the life out of respectable local folk with their rough ways and prodigious 'randies' or drinking sprees. The canal they built was a vital waterway for goods passing between London and Birmingham for the best part of half a century, until the railways arrived and captured most of its traffic. These days brightly painted narrowboats bump and bang through the locks with no more cargo than a handful of holidaymakers.

The fields just north of Bourne End were the scene of one of Britain's worst railway accidents, and one whose cause has never been explained. On a sunny September morning in 1945, Captain McCallum of the USAF was taking off from Bovingdon airfield, two miles away, when he glanced down and saw the night express from Perth plunge down the embankment and pile up in the fields below. Captain McCallum radioed for help, and the emergency services were soon on the scene, where they found a pile of wreckage 30 feet high. Forty-one passengers died, along with the driver and fireman. Why Driver Swaby had ignored warning signals and driven at 70 m.p.h. over a 20 m.p.h. crossing, no one knows to this day.

Go under the railway line (032063) and pass Winkworth Dock, full of narrowboats – some more like homes than means of transport, with TV aerials and flower boxes – to reach the red-tiled, flower-hung Three Horseshoes pub, built in 1535, looking at its own reflection in the canal by the swingbridge (027064). Turn left over a little brick bridge to meet the A41 (027063), where you turn right along the pavement for 400 yards to go left up a bridleway between the neighbouring bungalows of Farthings and Tara (023063). At a gate and stile (white arrow; golf course warning) keep straight ahead over a footbridge across the Berkhamsted bypass and straight up the slope of the golf course (footpath signs) with a fine view opening out along the Bulbourne Valley.

The following reflections will not please golfers – but one can't help thinking, as one walks these unnatural, shaven, too-green greens and fairways, of the farmland that should be here; or of the nature reserve that might have been established where now the wee white ball flies. Do golfers need to take up so much countryside, so close to London?

On the other hand, the Little Hay Golf Complex is at least egalitarian. There's no blackballing of 'unsuitable' applicants. Anyone who pays their fee can swing a club here.

One hundred and fifty yards past the club house, turn off the drive to the left (footpath sign) into woodland, to reach the B4505 (022047), where you turn right, then left in 400 yards just before the Bobsleigh Inn (011046 – footpath sign to Bovingdon). Turn right in 400 yards down a stony lane to reach Bovingdon church (017038).

'Unplanned aimlessness' fulminates R.M. Healey in his *Shell Guide to Hertfordshire*, 'crude . . . seedy'. Not at this end of the village, anyway, where old brick cottages cluster round the handsome, early Victorian, flint-built Church of St Lawrence in its four-acre churchyard. Don't miss the curious wooden memorial to Blanche and Thomas Green, standing like a cranky set of village stocks by the churchyard path.

Leave the churchyard through the south gate, turning left along Church Street and right over a stile in 50 yards where the road bends left (footpath sign). Cross three more stiles, and where a sign shows a crossroads of footpaths (021036) turn left and walk northeast along field edges for 1½ miles in enormous, rolling fields.

Woods come in on your left, and the path then crosses a field diagonally (032047) to a lane. Bear left past Felden Barns, then left again (037048 – footpath fingerpost) to skirt a field and the garden of Chichele Lodge (038050). Two metal kissing gates lead to a road, and a third in the hedge opposite to a lane through a mini golf course. Turn right to reach a road (040053); bear left downhill for 100 yards, then right into a stony lane opposite Hillside House (footpath sign). In 10 yards you can take the first side-turning, sloping downhill on the left to reach Hemel Hempstead station, but if you have some energy left, carry on up the lane, bearing left to reach Roughmoor Common above the trees.

The canal navvies camped on Roughmoor Common, too, and local people have picnicked here since time out of mind. A flock of Soay sheep grazes the common, part of a management process that has kept Roughmoor rich in wild flowers, butterflies and moths. The sheep are taken off the common between April and August to allow the orchids that flourish here to flower and set their seeds. Roughmoor is wild, open and lonely. What a perfect spot for a golf course . . .

14

Aldbury, Ashridge and Ivinghoe Beacon
(Herts/Bucks border)

INFORMATION

Map OS 1:50,000 Landranger Sheet 165 'Aylesbury and Leighton Buzzard'.

Travel
  Train (BR) – Tring.
  Car – A41 to Tring. Park at station.

Length of walk 8 miles – circular – start and finish at Tring BR station.

Conditions Chalk and grass tracks, much in woodland; gravelled paths. Parts can be slippery after rain. Take binoculars for view from Ivinghoe Beacon.

Opening times *Bridgewater Monument* Easter–September, Mondays–Thursdays 2–5, Saturdays and Sundays 2–5.30

Refreshments Greyhound or Valiant Trooper, Aldbury; Royal Hotel, Tring station.

Reading
  A Visitor's Guide to Aldbury by Jean Davis (from Aldbury village shop on the green).
  Aldbury by M. Webb (on sale in church).
  National Trust guide to the Ashridge Estate from Ashridge Pavilion by Bridgewater monument.

This walk is set at the outermost northern end of the Chiltern hills, where they make their final plunge into the flat plain where Hertfordshire meets Buckinghamshire. This is rolling, wooded countryside of cornfields and curving chalk ridges, where the influence of London is only whispered in the ranks of commuter cars in Tring station car park. As you walk north from the charming village of Aldbury, up through the woodlands of the Ashridge Estate, the views over the plain into Buckinghamshire and Oxfordshire widen all the way. They are exciting curtain-raisers for the dramatic panorama at 755 feet from the crest of Ivinghoe Beacon – one of the great views of southern England.

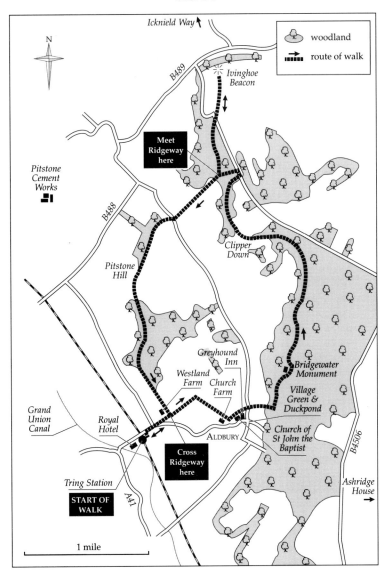

Icknield Way ↑

woodland
route of walk

Ivinghoe
Beacon

B489

Meet
Ridgeway
here

N

Pitstone
Cement
Works

B488

Clipper
Down

Pitstone
Hill

Greyhound
Inn

Westland
Farm

Church
Farm

Bridgewater
Monument

Village
Green &
Duckpond

Grand
Union
Canal

Royal
Hotel

ALDBURY

Church of
St John the
Baptist

B4506

Cross
Ridgeway
here

Tring Station

START OF
WALK

A41

Ashridge
House
→

1 mile

From Tring railway station (951122 – a mile east of the town) turn
right on to the road to Aldbury and in 150 yards ignore a turning
on the left to Pitstone and Ivinghoe. In another 100 yards turn left
(953124) up the driveway of Westland Farm ('Bridleway' and
'Ridgeway Path' signs). Continue ahead where the drive bends left,
to cross a stile. Here the Ridgeway is signposted, rising to the left;
but keep straight ahead (blue 'public bridleway' sign) through two
gates, along a narrow path between hedges of elder and sloe –

amateur wine-makers, take note. In ¼ mile a side track leads off to
the right over a stile (958127) between wooden fences, making for
the tower of Aldbury church. Crossing two more stiles, you turn
left over a third beside the corrugated iron barn of Church Farm
(962125) and cross a field to the left of a big, solitary ash tree.
Another stile brings you down across the school playing field to a
stile in the bottom right-hand corner, which lands you by the
much-photographed duck pond (965125) on Aldbury's delightful
village green.

Aldbury is the archetypal southern English village – pond, green and
trees overlooked by the early 16th-century Old Manor House, all
mellow brick and timber walls, whose stubby gable and mullioned,
latticed windows gaze at their reflection in the water. Behind the Old
Manor House rises the tall chimney of the old village bakehouse, built
over an ancient well, and over its shoulder peeps the grey flint tower of
the Church of St John the Baptist. The Pendley Chapel, in the south-
eastern corner, is the chief treasure of the church. Here lie Sir Robert
and Lady Whittingham, their beautifully carved effigies staring heaven-
wards with serene expressions. Sir Robert, who died in 1452, has no
customary lion nor mastiff for a footrest, but a shaggy-limbed, straggle-
bearded wild man of the woods, girdled with ivy and clutching a
knotted club, who also gazes up into glory with his heathen head
supported on one hand.

Back at the pond, walk up the road signposted 'Ivinghoe', past
the creeper-hung Greyhound Inn, and in 150 yards turn right up
a gravelly track (965126) opposite a thatched row of half-timbered
almshouses. The path rises into the woods, bearing right on entering the trees to meet a sunken, chalky lane. Turn left here and
follow the lane as it climbs in the dappled shade of beech and pine
trees – a typical Chiltern woodland track, knobbly with tree roots
and floored with chunks of chalk and flint. There are fine views
between the trees, over Tring station and the milky earth of rolling
ploughland under dark cushions of woods, as you mount to a clearing (971131) where the Bridgewater Monument rears its fluted
100-foot column over the countryside.

'In honour of Francis, Third Duke of Bridgewater, "Father of Inland
Navigation", 1832' runs the inscription on the monument. But the
Duke – by all accounts a bloody-minded and autocratic individual –
owed much of his success as a pioneer of canal building in the mid-
18th century to his engineer James Brindley, an untutored practical
genius, unable to write or draw properly but blessed with vision and an
endless capacity to overcome obstacles by common sense and hard
work. The two men built Britain's first canal in 1761 to carry coal to
Manchester from the Duke's mines at Worsley in Lancashire. Others

followed, including the Grand Junction Canal (1793–1806) which now runs as the Grand Union Canal a few hundred yards from Tring station.

From the top of the monument, 170 steps up, you can enjoy a superb view over many miles of Herts, Beds, Bucks and Oxfordshire as well as a glimpse eastward over the massed trees of the Duke's Ashridge Estate. Here lies the enormous Gothic mansion of Ashridge House, designed by the great architect James Wyatt in 1808, its grounds laid out by the equally celebrated Capability Brown, its gardens by his pupil Humphry Repton, all to the orders of the Duke of Bridgewater's heir, the seventh Earl. Thousands of acres of beautiful mature woodland all round the house are now in the care of the National Trust and open to the public.

On the far side of the monument the path (signed 'Nature Trail'), follows the curves of the hillside for a couple of miles. The wooded face and grassy green dome of Clipper Down are seen ahead through gaps in the trees, and soon the bridleway hurdles the neck of the down (963147) to reach the open backbone of the Ivinghoe Hills at a road (963156). After admiring the view, turn sharply back to take the path ('public footpath' sign) 15 yards on your left, which descends between bushes of may and blackthorn to meet the Ridgeway path at a stile (961155), with a view ahead of the sprawling buildings and tall chimneys of the unlovely Pitstone cement works in the valley. Turn right along the Ridgeway and keep straight ahead for ½ mile to cross the road (960163) and climb to the summit of Ivinghoe Beacon (960168).

Two great and ancient trackways meet at Ivinghoe Beacon – the Ridgeway, which has come 90 miles north-east from Avebury in Wiltshire, striding the hard chalk tops of the hills, and the Icknield Way that takes up the route and carries it on along the sides of hills capped with sticky clay for another 100 miles into Suffolk, where it hands over to the Peddars Way for a final 50-mile run to the north Norfolk coast near Hunstanton.

From the 755-foot brow of Ivinghoe Beacon, standing amidst a number of prehistoric monuments – an Iron Age fort and a Bronze Age barrow among them – you look out over miles of countryside, patched yellow with corn, green with pasture and brown with ploughland, to where the Oxfordshire plain shades off into the blue of extreme distance. Model gliders swoop on the thermals, and children turn cartwheels of delight in the scrubby turf. This is a long moment to savour.

From the Beacon, retrace your steps to where you joined the Ridgeway path, then swing right and descend to cross a plateau of cornfields by a stile (959153) and a road (954150) before setting your back to the Pitstone cement works and striding the airy spine

of Pitstone Hill among ancient, stunted thorn trees. The path bears left round the corner of a field, then right along the edge of a wood to pick up the Ridgeway again at a stile into the trees (950139). You cross Duchie's Piece, a small area of open chalk grassland managed for wild flowers and butterflies by the Herts and Middlesex Wildlife Trust, and shortly afterwards meet a bridlepath (951131) where you turn right, then left in 200 yards along the bottom of the woodland. Within ¼ mile you will find yourself back at the Ridgeway signpost above Westlands Farm (954124), where you turn right over the stile to reach the road and Tring station.

15

Pegsdon and the Icknield Way
on Telegraph Hill
(Herts/Beds border)

INFORMATION

Map OS 1:50,000 Landranger Sheet 166 'Luton and Hertford'.

Travel CAR – M25 to Jct 21; M1 to Jct 10 (Luton Airport); A1081; A505 towards Hitchin; 1 mile from Hitchin, minor road on left (Pirton sign); in ½ mile turn left on B655 to Pegsdon (2½ miles). Park at Live and Let Live Inn.

Length of walk 6 miles – figure-of-eight – start and finish at Live and Let Live Inn. ✂ *Short cuts* – including both short cuts 3½ miles; including short cut [1] 4½ miles; including short cut [2] 5 miles.

Conditions The Icknield Way, and paths crossing fields, can be very sticky and wet after rain.

Refreshments Live and Let Live Inn, Pegsdon.

Reading

    The Icknield Way Path, guidebook published by Icknield Way Association.

    The Icknield Way by Edward Thomas.

    Pilgrim's Progress by John Bunyan.

Two entirely contrasting landscapes delight you on this walk – the lumpy chalk hills of the escarpment at the extreme north-west edge of Hertfordshire, and the great undulating clay plain of Bedfordshire that stretches at their feet. The ancient high-level track of the Icknield Way runs like a thread across these chalk downs, celebrated by writers as famous as John Bunyan and Edward Thomas, and as obscure as G.M. Boumphrey, a 1930s travel writer now entirely forgotten but equally stunned by the view over Bedfordshire from the Hertfordshire heights.

Standing under the pub sign of the Live and Let Live Inn (121302), turn right, then left just before the B655 down the private road to Pegsdon Common Farm for 300 yards; then go right (126305 – footpath sign) and climb beside a small wood (yellow arrow), dog-legging across fields and admiring the view.

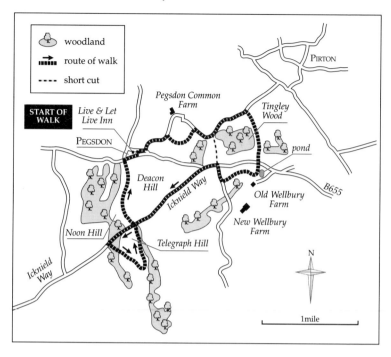

To your left, the Bedfordshire clay lands sweep away for 15 miles to the horizon, well-hedged and wooded blue-brown soil dotted with villages and solitary farms. In contrast, the hillsides where you are walking bulge and billow in the characteristic shapes of chalk downs. The flank of the escarpment is deeply gashed by dry valleys, flushed out of the chalk by springs long dried up, their sides thick with thorny scrub on the close cropped turf where sheep graze. Beech and ash woods stand out against the sky on the tops of these beautiful and exhilarating downs, the last effort of the Chilterns before subsiding into clay and flatness.

Turn left along a bridleway at the crest (132305) and bear left at a fork in 120 yards (blue arrow) (✂ *short cut* [1] – bear right to rejoin walk at the B655). The bridleway begins to descend towards Pirton village ahead; blue arrows on a wooden post point forward (140310), but turn right here (yellow arrow) to skirt Tingley Wood and descend to the B655 (141301). Turn left for 15 yards, then right (footpath sign) up a field edge, keeping a hedge and then a tree-encircled pond on your left, to bear right above Old Wellbury Farm crouched in its hollow and make for a yellow arrow waymark at the top corner of the field (139299). Follow arrows across a field to turn right along the drive from New Wellbury Farm, then left along the B655 (134301) (✂ *short cut* [1] – rejoins here).

In 200 yards, just past the Bedfordshire county boundary sign ('A Progressive County') turn left on to the Icknield Way path.

The Icknield Way has brought travellers north and east from the Wiltshire plains into East Anglia for at least 6,000 years – probably more. Here the Way climbs the gentle slope of Telegraph Hill, the site of one of the semaphore stations set up in the 18th century by the Admiralty at 10-mile intervals between Great Yarmouth and London, to signal news of events both routine and epoch-making, the victory at the Battle of Trafalgar among them. The supreme country writer Edward Thomas, in his book *The Icknield Way* (1913), described this stretch to perfection:

> 'The Icknield Way took a south-westerly course, and mounted steeply up as a green, almost rutless lane between high hedges. It was green and even as soon as it left the hard road, and now for the first time made a real bold ascent of the chalk . . . There were daisies all over it, and roses hung upon either side. Nearing the hill-top it narrowed, and had steep banks on the left with brambles and thorns over them. But right to the top it kept those high hedges.'

Keep to the Icknield Way over the crest of Telegraph Hill (✄ *short cut* [2] – turn right through hedge at 120290, and walk down to Pegsdon). Half-way down the slope turn left (116287 – blue arrow) on a track that climbs over the back of Telegraph Hill. In ⅓ mile turn left along a green trackway (122284) to rejoin the Icknield Way (120290); turn right, and in 25 yards go left through the hedge (as short cut [2]) to the edge of the dry valley under Noon Hill.

These chalk hills above the plain were John Bunyan's inspiration when he wrote in *Pilgrim's Progress* of the Delectable Mountains, which Christian saw far off from Palace Beautiful, and from whose peak called Clear he and Hopeful had their first glimpse of the Celestial City. G.M. Boumphrey, in his now unremembered book *Along The Roman Roads* (1935), described coming unexpectedly on this immense view:

> 'On Pegsdon Barn you are standing on the northern brink of the chalk downs; immediately in front of you the turf sweeps down three hundred feet; and beyond that spread miles and miles of Bedfordshire, Buckinghamshire and Cambridgeshire, utterly unspoilt as yet . . . unrecognizable miles and miles of country. It is a grand spot and one can understand the impression it must have made on John Bunyan.'

Keep to the left-hand brink of the deep dry valley on your right, and follow the yellow arrows down the face of the Delectable Mountains to the B655 and Pegsdon.

16

Ayot St Lawrence
and the Ayot Greenway
(Herts)

INFORMATION

Map OS 1:50, 000 Landranger Sheet 166 'Luton and Hertford'.
Travel CAR – M25 to Jct 23; A1(M) north to A1000 (Welwyn turn-off); follow signs to Welwyn (NB – *not* to Welwyn Garden City); turn right into main village street and pass church; at roundabout turn left down Fulling Mill Lane (Ayot St Lawrence sign); in 1½ miles turn left to Ayot St Lawrence. Park at Brocket Arms.
Length of walk 5½ miles – circular – start and finish at Brocket Arms pub.
Conditions Last mile of walk on very muddy bridleway – otherwise good underfoot.
Opening Times Shaw's Corner April–end October, Wednesdays –Saturdays 2–6; Sundays and Bank Holidays 12–6.
Refreshments Brocket Arms, Ayot St Lawrence.

The sprawl of Welwyn Garden City lies only three miles to the east, but these quiet miles of walking through the Hertfordshire farmlands are pleasantly rural in character. You start from one of the best pubs in England, visit an eccentric church that commemorates a bygone marital squabble, walk where the steam trains once clanked, and finish with an exploration of the house of one of Ireland's greatest writers.

From the Brocket Arms (196168) turn left down the village street for 200 yards to find the ruins of an abandoned church on your right. From the following bend in the road a path runs to the right over fields to bring you to the neo-classical Church of St Lawrence (191169).

Parts of the Brocket Arms in Ayot St Lawrence date back to Tudor times, and may be earlier. This is a pearl of a pub – an adventurous

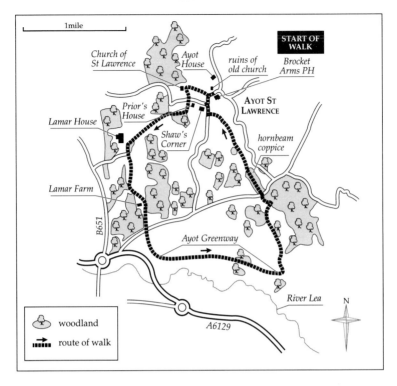

START OF WALK

Church of St Lawrence

Ayot House

ruins of old church

Brocket Arms PH

AYOT ST LAWRENCE

Prior's House

Lamar House

Shaw's Corner

hornbeam coppice

Lamar Farm

B651

Ayot Greenway

River Lea

N

A6129

woodland

route of walk

1 mile

selection of well-kept beers, good food in restaurant or bar, open fires in cold weather, beams and dark nooks enough and to spare.

In the 1770s a rich baronet could do pretty much what he pleased. It was an autocratic decision that ruined Ayot's old church, and another that saw the new one built. Sir Lyonel Lyde of Ayot House, a tobacco merchant from Bristol, began to demolish the 14th-century church because it was blocking the view from his house. When the Bishop of Lincoln slapped an injunction on the despoiler, he had to stay his hand; but the new Palladian church was built to his orders and finished in 1778. With its verdigris copper roof, colonnaded porch and flanking pavilions it resembles a Greek temple, a bizarre note in the gentle Hertfordshire countryside. The interior is flawless, a simple and tasteful design in white and blue. Sir Lyonel had the altar sited at the western end so that the grand entrance portico could face his house across the park – perhaps to cock a snook at the bishop as well.

The tombs of Sir Lyonel and his wife stand one in each of the side pavilions, as far apart as possible. The story is that they squabbled throughout their marriage; and the peppery baronet decreed that, having been forced together by the church in life, he would at least make sure they were separated by it in death.

Turn left down the pathway from the church to reach a road (191168); turn right, then left just past Prior's House over a stile (footpath sign) into a wood. Turn right (yellow arrow), then bear left where the trees end (189166) along an avenue of lime trees, to turn left (182161) down the driveway of Lamar House.

Here lived Apsley Cherry Garrard, author of _The Worst Journey In The World_, his graphic account of his participation in the doomed 1912 expedition of Captain Scott to the South Pole.

In 100 yards, where the drive bends right, keep ahead on a rough track for ¼ mile. Enter trees, and go left through a tall gate (182153) through trees and across a field, bearing right above the sheds of Lamar Farm on to a stony path which crosses a road (184148 – stile, yellow arrow and 'Marford' footpath sign) to descend and turn left for 1¼ miles along the Ayot Greenway (186144).

The Greenway.runs along a section of the disused Luton, Dunstable and Welwyn Junction Railway line, opened in 1860 and closed to passengers in 1965. The railway relied largely on the transport of new cars from the Vauxhall factory at Luton, and died when they began to be moved by road. Hertfordshire County Council bought up this 2½ mile stretch in 1978, and has made a good job of converting it into a bridleway, cycle track and footpath. Parts are embanked, with wide views over gently rolling countryside; other sections run in cuttings, enclosing you in a green tunnel of ash and hawthorn loud with birdsong.

Just before a bridge over the railway (204142), a post on the left marked 'Access to Footpath' points up the side of the cutting. Beside the bridge turn left (yellow arrow) across the fields. In 300 yards keep ahead to the left of a little wood; at the end of the wood (204149) aim ahead for the right-hand corner of another wood (203150), and follow it, then a hedge, to the right to reach a gate (203152). Turn left to cross a road and continue along a track (bridleway sign), avoiding the mire by crossing a stile on the right and walking through a hornbeam wood carefully coppiced and managed by the Herts and Essex Wildlife Trust. Rejoin the bridleway (200157) and follow it back to Ayot St Lawrence, emerging on the road just below Shaw's Corner (194166).

George Bernard Shaw, the passionate socialist Irish playwright and polemicist, settled in what was then the New Rectory in 1906 when he was 50, and lived there until his death in 1950 at the ripe old age of 94. Here, among many other famous works, he wrote _Pygmalion_ (later to be popularised as _My Fair Lady_) and _St Joan_. In 1925, the year after _St Joan_, he was awarded the Nobel Prize for Literature.

Shaw presented the house to the National Trust, and you can end your walk by wandering through the study where he wrote, the summer house where he would hole up with his typewriter to get away from distractions (though not from the telephone – one was installed there), and the garden where his ashes were scattered.

Hertingfordbury and the Cole Greenway
(Herts)

INFORMATION

Map OS 1:50,000 Landranger Sheet 166 'Luton and Hertford'.
Travel
 TRAIN (BR) – Hertford North.
 CAR – M25 to Jct 25; A10 to A414 Hertford junction; A414
  for 2 miles; A602 Stevenage road for ⅓ mile to Hertford
  North station. Park opposite station.
Length of walk 7 miles – circular – start and finish at Hertford
 North station (✂ *short cut* – 5½ miles).
Conditions Lanes, field paths, old railway line converted to
 bridleway.
Refreshments Sele Arms, opposite Hertford North station; White
 Horse, Hertingfordbury; Cowper Arms, Cole Green.
Reading
 Hertingfordbury church and village notes, available in St
  Mary's Church, Hertingfordbury.
 Cole Greenway pamphlet, from Hertfordshire County
  Council.

This walk in a peaceful corner of Hertfordshire is coloured by memories of times past – a dubious murder trial at the turn of the 18th century; the great house, now vanished, where the defendant's family held sway for centuries; a path along a disused railway line now enjoying a new lease of life as a storehouse of nature; a lovely old farmstead by the River Lea on a site occupied for at least a thousand years.

From Hertford North station (317129) turn right along North Road for 100 yards, then right up steps (footpath sign). In 70 yards a footpath sign ('Chelmsford Wood ¾') leads you over the railway to turn left for ½ mile and descend to a section of disused road above the A414 (310124). Turn right to cross the dual carriageway (with great care!) and walk down an old slip road into leafy Hertingfordbury.

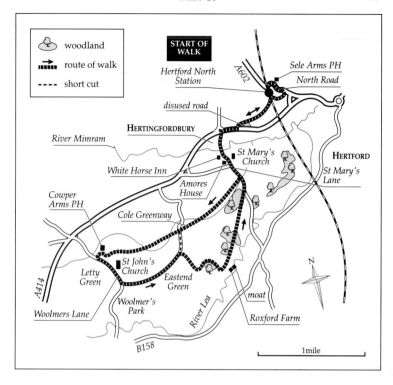

'One of the prettiest villages in the county' said a Hertfordshire historian in 1728, and his judgement still applies. Attractive old cottages line the village street, which leads past the White Horse, a handsome white-painted inn dating back in part to Tudor times. On the corner of St Mary's Lane stands Amores House, even older than the White Horse; and up the lane is St Mary's Church (309120) with its imposing tower and yew-crowded churchyard.

The interior of the church was thoroughly but imaginatively restored in Victorian times. Its chief interest lies in its splendid collection of monuments; but before examining these, note the two certificates dated 1770 under the tower arch, declaring that Eleanor Watts and Sarah Porter had been buried in woollen shrouds – a legal requirement at that time, to help boost England's flagging wool trade.

Elaborate iron gates guard the Cowper Chapel, where a superb life-size winged Victory and a distraught cherub do honour to the second Lord Cowper of Panshanger Park. In the north wall two graceful figures – a blindfold, nubile Justice and a helmeted Wisdom – flank the seated, pensive Spencer Cowper, a judge who in his young days was charged with the murder of Sarah Stout, a Quaker woman who was found drowned after a visit from him. She probably committed suicide after Cowper had broken off their relationship. The trial in 1699 was a farce, in which Cowper was acquitted after the judge forgot the evidence and felt too faint to sum up for the jury. As a judge himself in later years, the chastened Cowper was noted for his reluctance to inflict death sentences.

By the south porch stands a headstone to a plain-speaking Hertingfordbury publican who died in 1853:

> 'Too stern in truth to practise polish'd ease,
> And blandness, which means any thing you please,
> One plain unvarnish'd course JOHN BENTLEY ran,
> And better heart ne'er glow'd in mortal man . . .
> O God have mercy! Shield us from the snare
> Of sudden death like his. Beware! Beware!'

From the church turn left along St Mary's Lane, under a railway bridge (309116) and immediately left up on to the railway line, where you turn left to walk for 1½ miles to Cole Green (✂ *short cut* – ¾ mile along the Cole Greenway, climb to a road bridge and turn left to rejoin the walk at Eastend Green).

In 1974 Hertfordshire County Council bought this section of the old line from Hertford to Welwyn Garden City (opened in 1858, closed to passengers in 1951 and to goods in 1966), and established the Cole Greenway along it. This is a delightful path snaking through wooded, gently swelling countryside, a haven for birds – warblers, finches, black-caps, tits – who forage among the hips and haws, sloes and hazelnuts of the banks, where sections of scrub have been cleared to create flowery grassland. Cole Green station was provided specially for the Cowper family of Panshanger Park, a huge Gothic mansion – now demolished – built nearby in 1800 with grounds enclosed from local farmland (to the fury of local farmers) and landscaped by Humphry Repton.

At Cole Green station site (285111) leave the railway through the car park on the right, to turn left beside the Cowper Arms, under the line and into Letty Green.

St John's Church at the crossroads (286109), flint-built in 1849, contains a little stained glass window to Cecilia, Countess of Strathmore and grandmother to Queen Elizabeth II who often came to church here when staying as a child at the Strathmores' nearby house of Woolmers. The window shows St Cecilia holding a pipe organ, her fingers ready to squeeze the bellows.

From the church turn left down Woolmers Lane, past the gate to the house and on for ¾ mile to the lonely hamlet of Eastend Green, a few handsome houses along grassy verges (✂ *short cut* – rejoins here). Go right by a pond hollow (297108 – 'Roxford' sign) along

a path between bushes, to turn right in 50 yards over a stile and down a field edge. Follow yellow arrows as you dog-leg across fields down into the wide valley of the River Lea where you reach Roxford Farm (303104).

Roxford is a fine big house under red tiles, with large windows full of tiny square panes, some shuttered. It's charmingly situated among trees, with an ancient moated site between house and river. *Domesday Book* mentions 'Rochesforde', and the farmstead seems likely to outlast the clattering gravel works just along the river and return one day to its immemorial peace.

Turn left above the house ('St Mary's Lane' bridleway fingerpost) and follow the path for ⅔ mile to St Mary's Lane (309115), where you turn left under the Cole Greenway for Hertingfordbury, the A414 crossing and the footpath by Chelmsford Wood back to Hertford North station.

·18·

Monken Hadley
Common
(Middlesex)

INFORMATION

Map OS 1:50,000 Landranger Sheet 176 'West London'.
Travel
    TUBE – Cockfosters (Piccadilly line).
    CAR – M25 to Jct 24; A111 towards London. Park at
      Cockfosters station (3 miles).
Length of walk 4 miles – circular – start and finish at
    Cockfosters station.
Conditions Side roads and woodland paths, some muddy.
    You might like to take a compass for direction-finding on
    Monken Hadley Common, though commonsense will keep
    you on the right track.
Refreshments Cock and Dragon Inn, Games Road, Cockfosters.
    West Lodge Park Hotel, Hadley Wood (on A121 1½ miles N.
    of Cockfosters station) for beer and sandwiches, or full
    restaurant meal, in luxurious surroundings.
Reading Local history section at Palmers Green Library,
    Bromfield Lane, Palmers Green (081 982–7453) is very
    helpful.

There is no set route among the trees, streams and bushes of Monken Hadley Common – you can take your pick of any number of sinuous paths that will bring you back safely to your starting point. This is a walk to savour slowly, wandering through this slip of wilderness where north London meets the Hertfordshire countryside, a tiny green remnant of a once mighty royal hunting forest.

From Cockfosters station (281964) cross the A111 Cockfosters Road into Chalk Lane, which bends right by Christ Church to reach a T-junction with Games Road (279967). Turn left here, with the Cock and Dragon Inn on your left, and walk along to the eastern end of Monken Hadley Common, where a path runs along the southern border.

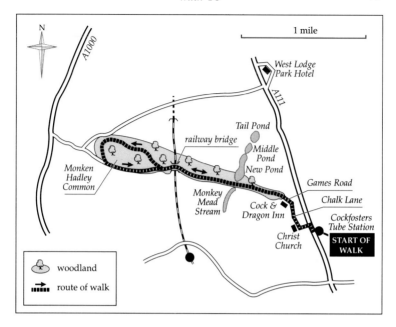

A notice on the common announces that it is open to the public for 'quiet enjoyment', and asks wanderers to maintain common and woods 'in that clean and pleasant state in which you would wish to find them'. Unnecessary pleading in this prosperous suburb of north London, perhaps, but a reminder of how much local people value this long, thin triangle of oak-studded common land with its thickets of holly, beeches, ponds and marshy hollows.

'These are pretty retreats for gentlemen, especially those who are studious and lovers of privacy,' remarked the diarist John Evelyn in the 1670s, half a century after King James I had been the last monarch to hunt what were then the vast tracts of the royal forest of Enfield Chase. But even in Evelyn's day the woodland of the Chase was being eroded by local peasants felling trees and ploughing up the land for agriculture. A hundred years after the diarist recorded his impressions of Enfield Chase, King George III gave in to demands by keen agriculturalists and by rich London merchants on the look-out for land on which to build their country estates, and agreed in 1777 to an Act of Enclosure which soon saw the Chase sold off in small sections for farmland or development. The local commoners or 'stintholders' were given parcels of their own land in compensation.

Luckily for our generation, the stintholders of the village of Monken Hadley couldn't agree on a fair distribution of their allotments of Enfield Chase land, and the Monken Hadley portion of the Chase ended up in trust, where it remains. Hence the survival of the common as unbuilt-upon, unviolated wild country.

The path descends with suburban houses on the left and the tree-crowded common on the right, to reach a bridge over a stream (271969). Turn right here to find the common's string of ponds.

There are three of these ponds going north across the common – New Pond, Middle Pond and Tail Pond – favourite haunts of fishermen and of seagulls, moorhens and ducks. The stream that connects them is known as Monkey Mead – 'the meadow of the monks' – recalling a hermitage established in this corner of Enfield Chase long before Norman times.

The path runs on from the bridge up an avenue of crazily tilted trees to cross a railway line (263971) and descend through a gate to an open green space on the right. Walk across this clearing and bear left among the trees, following whichever path you choose.

There is a delicious feeling of solitude in this secluded little wood, only a couple of hundred yards deep and perhaps half a mile long. Holly thickets and bramble bushes stand under the oaks, interspersed every now and then with patches of grass as reminders of the days when all this area of common land was extensively grazed by the stintholders' animals. The stintholders had the right to gather the 'underwood' or scrub wood for house building and domestic fires, and there was an ancient right of wayfaring which meant that anyone could cross the Chase – some of the tangled paths hereabouts are rights of way many centuries old.

Monken Hadley stintholders still have the right to pasture their animals on the common – a right no longer used. 'But one day someone will exercise their right,' the Curator of the Monken Hadley Common Trustees told me, 'and then it'll bring the traffic from the M25 to a standstill' – a delightful thought.

Make an anti-clockwise circuit of the western end of the common, using the stream that flows through it as a guide or simply trusting to your judgement. All paths will eventually bring you back to the track along the southern edge of the common, along which you can then retrace your steps back to Chalk Lane and Cockfosters station.

Essendon and
Little Berkhamsted
(Herts)

INFORMATION

Map OS 1:50,000 Landranger Sheet 166 'Luton and Hertford'.
Travel
>   Car – M25 to Jct 24; A111 and A1000 towards Hatfield; in
>   2½ miles, B158 to Essendon. Park near Salisbury Crest
>   pub.
>   Bus – Green Line (Victoria) 081 668–7261. Local
>   information: 0923 257405. London Victoria–Hatfield
>   Market Place–Essendon; buses stop near church or
>   Salisbury Crest pub.

Length of walk 3½ miles – circular – start and finish at Salisbury
Crest pub, Essendon.
Conditions A mixture of farm tracks, surfaced golf course paths,
green roads – and one exceptionally muddy bridleway
(which can be outflanked).
Opening Times *St Mary's Church Essendon* during British
Summer Time (3rd weekend in March–3rd weekend in
October), 10–5.
Refreshments Salisbury Crest, Essendon; Five Horseshoes, Little
Berkhamsted.
Reading Essendon church pamphlets, available in St Mary's
Church.

This short walk packs a great deal of interest into its couple of
hours. There's the pretty village of Little Berkhamsted with its weatherboarded cottages and cricket ground, the enormous red brick pile
where the founder of the Whitbread brewing fortunes once lived, a
couple of excellent Hertfordshire pubs and a very rare example of a font
from the famous Wedgwood pottery. Two eccentric constructions –
one low, one high – are included for good measure.

Just along the street from Essendon's Salisbury Crest pub (273088)
stands St Mary's Church, neatly repaired after a stray bomb, dropped

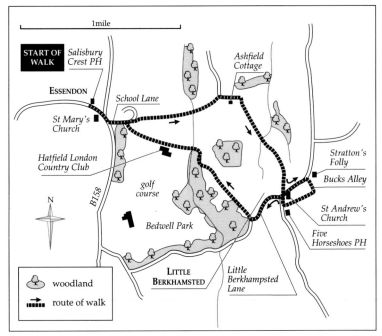

on 3rd September 1916 from a Zeppelin airship, destroyed its east end. The enormously rich and philanthropic 18th-century brewer Samuel Whitbread spent a good part of his fortune improving the village, and one of his sisters presented St Mary's in 1778 with a treasure – a superb black basalt font, crafted at the Wedgwood pottery in Stoke-on-Trent, its rim hung with moulded drapery swags. It is one of only two known to be in existence. The font has to be kept under lock and key in these vandalistic days, but you can view it by arrangement with the church key-holder.

Against the churchyard fence, SSW of the tower, lies a low table tomb inscribed with the name of one of Essendon's past rectors, the Reverend Robert Orme. The western end of the tomb is closed with a sheet of metal, which replaced the door put there on the orders of Mr Orme. He died in 1843, three days after his 83rd birthday, haunted by the fear of being buried while still alive. Certain precautions were laid down before his death to give him a chance if that eventuality – surprisingly common in those days – should come to pass. The coffin was entombed above ground, and in it were placed a bottle of wine, a loaf of bread and the key to the door in the tomb. The village worthies took no chances, either – they waited 38 years before finally sealing the door.

From the church turn right and walk along the B158, turning left along School Lane (275086) and down a paved path (footpath sign) across a golf course.

There have been brave attempts at landscaping the golf course – conifers and ornamental trees planted, lakes dug, curly little paths laid out. But shouldn't such a development, spreading as it does over so much landscape, go hand in hand with conservation? Those ridges of rough ground between the fairways would be perfect for butterflies if sensitively managed, and the barren lakes could teem with dragonflies and frogs if the appropriate vegetation were encouraged. Thousands of acres around London are being converted into golf courses, each one an opportunity waiting for some conservationist's energy and inspiration.

Cross a watersplash (282087) and climb to turn right along a farm road (285089). Pass weatherboarded Ashfield Cottage and bear right (288089) into an exceptionally muddy bridleway. A footpath along the field edge to the left, reached by a stile, offers a better footing to walk down into the valley, cross the stream and climb to a stile (292082). Turn right to reach a road (292080), where you turn left for 250 yards towards the tall tower of Stratton's Folly (295081).

The castellated round brick tower, 100 feet high, was built in 1789 by John Stratton for reasons now obscure. Probably he used it as an observatory; but local legend made out that he wanted to keep an eye on his ships in the River Thames, 20 miles south as the crow flies – rather a tall order!

Turn right in front of the tower, along Bucks Alley, and in 150 yards right over a stile (footpath fingerpost) along the edge of two fields to reach St Andrew's Church in Little Berkhamsted (292079).

The 17th-century church with its weatherboarded tower and broach spire stands opposite an attractive row of old cottages and next to the Five Horseshoes pub, a good place to put your feet up. Opposite the pub is the village cricket ground – appropriately enough, since Brian 'Jonners' Johnston, the celebrated cricket commentator, was born in the village.

From the Five Horseshoes turn right past the church and left at the war memorial along Little Berkhampstead Lane. In 300 yards, after two bends, turn right (289077 – bridleway sign) along a driveway and green lane.

There's a fine view to your left of the long brick pile of Bedwell Park, once the home of Samuel Whitbread. He was a dedicated social reformer, putting his brewing money to work supporting his ideals. But he ended his life crushed in despair of ever putting right the ignorance, poverty and disease so widespread in Georgian Britain.

Descend through horse chestnut woods and turn left through a kissing gate (283084) to bear right round the vast, overblown Hatfield London Country Club (terracotta maidens strewing roses on the terrace, life-size beefeater effigies at the door) on a path that runs uphill (277086). Turn left, and right along the B158 to return to the Salisbury Crest pub.

20

Roydon and
Hunsdon Mead
(Herts/Essex border)

INFORMATION

Map OS 1:50,000 Landranger Sheet 167 'Chelmsford and
  Harlow'.
Travel
  TRAIN (BR) – Roydon.
  CAR – M25 to Jct 25; A10 towards Hertford for 7 miles;
    A414 to Stanstead Abbotts; B181 to Roydon. Park near
    station.
Length of walk 2½ miles – circular – start and finish at Roydon
  station.
Conditions Towpath and field tracks. Take flower book.
Refreshments White Horse, Roydon.
Reading *Hunsdon Mead* Wildside Walk leaflet from Essex
  County Council Planning Department, County Hall,
  Chelmsford, Essex.

Though one of the shortest walks in this book, this is one of the most
fascinating. St Peter's Church in Roydon is full of treasures, Roydon
itself is a pretty village to explore, and the Stort Navigation offers marvellous waterside walking. And if you take your walk in summer, you'll
find Hunsdon Mead a rare example of a traditional English meadow
crammed with wild flowers.

**From Roydon station (405105) go over the level crossing and turn
left immediately beside the bridge along the bank of the Stort
Navigation, walking through an underpass below the railway line
(408105) to reach Roydon Lock (410105).**

Through the bridge on the left flows the River Stort, while the lock
gates on the right give access to a loop cut for the convenience of barges
when the river was improved in the 18th century to become the Stort
Navigation canal. The canal was opened in 1766, to join up with the
River Lea just west of Roydon and take goods down to the Thames and

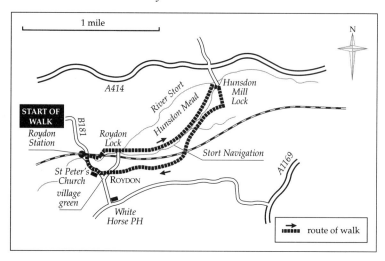

London. It enjoyed about 80 years of bustling commerce until the railway arrived and stole its trade. Now, fringed with reeds and overhung with hawthorn and willows, it makes a beautiful towpath walk.

Continue from the lock along the towpath on the left bank of the canal for about ½ mile; then get your flower book out and take a closer look at Hunsdon Mead, the large flat meadow on your left.

Islanded between the River Stort and the Stort Navigation, Hunsdon Mead becomes a sheet of flood water every winter, the feeding ground of golden plover and lapwings. Local people enjoy ancient rights of grazing on the meadow; and Roydon farmer, David Abbey, like his father before him, runs sheep and cattle here each autumn and winter, then leaves nature to her own devices from March until August when he cuts the hay. This traditional management results in a superb growth of wild flowers, uncontaminated by artificial herbicides or fertilisers. You'll find primroses, cowslips and marsh marigolds in spring; several species of orchids and the once common but now rare yellow rattle in summer. Compare the richness of Hunsdon Mead with the chemical green of the meadows on the other side of the canal to see just what we have lost through modern intensive farming methods.

Cross the lock gates of Hunsdon Mill Lock at the top of the meadow (421113), and return along the opposite bank of the canal. At a footbridge (420110) the path leaves the canal to cross the railway (418105 – take care and look both ways!). Turn right and walk beside the railway to dog-leg left and right, over a stile and beside gardens to reach the village green in Roydon (409102).

Opposite you is the tiny wooden shed, dark and cheerless, in which malefactors were once locked up for the night; and next to it stand the village stocks in which they were put on show for the admonition – and delight – of the good folk of Roydon.

Nearby is the 13th-century St Peter's Church, its walls a jumble of Roman tiles, flints, stones, chalk lumps and blocks of ashlar. Inside there's a fine old font carved with the heads of the four evangelists, each one a lively portrait of one of the inhabitants of medieval Roydon who helped to build St Peter's. Under the carpet in the chancel is a well-preserved brass to Sir Thomas and Lady Joan Colte. At the siege of Ludlow during the Wars of the Roses, Sir Thomas bravely took on a bunch of attackers from the Lancastrian side while his master the Duke of York escaped. He was later rewarded with a good slice of land around Roydon.

From the church turn right up the village street to find the White Horse pub; or left to return to the station.

21

Much Hadham
and Perry Green
(Herts)

INFORMATION

Map OS 1:50,000 Landranger Sheet 167 'Chelmsford and
  Harlow'.
Travel CAR – M25 to Jct 27; M11 north to Jct 8;
  A120 round Bishop's Stortford and on to Little Hadham;
  turn left in village to Much Hadham (2 miles). Park at
  St Andrew's Church.
Length of walk 5 miles – circular – start and finish at St
  Andrew's Church.
Conditions Bridleways, field paths and lanes. Bridleways very
  muddy in woodland.
Opening Times
  Henry Moore Foundation, Perry Green by prior arrangement
    only. Tel: 0279 843333.
  Much Hadham Forge open during working day.
  Forge Museum, Much Hadham Saturdays 10–4, Sundays
    12–4.
Refreshments The Bull, Much Hadham; Hoops Inn, Perry
  Green.
Reading
  Much Hadham church pamphlet, available in St Andrew's.
  Henry Moore Foundation – booklet available at the
    Foundation, Danetree House, Perry Green.

Man's ability to blend craftsmanship and artistry is the keynote of this
walk in and around the well-favoured Hertfordshire village of Much
Hadham – stonemasonry of the highest order in St Andrew's Church,
a marvellous assembly of houses spanning the architectural styles of
many centuries, the clink of a blacksmith's hammer in the village forge
– and, high on a ridge a couple of miles away, a superb collection of
pieces by the celebrated 20th-century master sculptor Henry Moore.

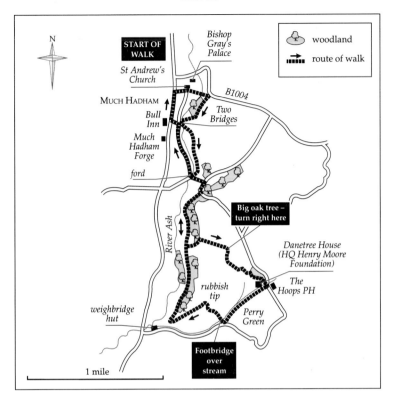

The Church of St Andrew in Much Hadham contains many treasures, chief among them the carvings by medieval masons. On the corbels holding up the nave roof timbers are grotesque, lively figures of a king, a woman with a spindle, a soldier with a great strap across his chest and various improbable-looking beasts. Angel musicians gaze sublimely from the south porch roof. Flanking the tower doorway are the hollow-eyed heads of a king and queen, presented to St Andrew's by Henry Moore, a parishioner for over 40 years.

Just north of the church stands Bishop Gray's Palace, nearly 600 years old, encased in red brick and gables in the late 17th century. Here in 1430 'Edmund of Hadham' was born, son of King Henry V's widow Katherine and her second husband Owen Tudor, her Clerk of the Wardrobe. Edmund was to father one of England's most effective kings, the dynamic Henry VII.

Another story attaching to Hadham church concerns the choleric Catholic Bishop Bonner in the 1550s. Riding through Much Hadham, Bonner was so infuriated at hearing no welcoming bells from the church tower, and at discovering that the 'popish' altar cross and candlesticks had been removed, that he lashed out with his fist at the rector, Edmund Brygett – but landed his blow on another man's ear by mistake. Bonner then rode on, still in a rage, while his chaplains stayed behind to enjoy the feast that had been laid out for him, laughing heartily at their master's discomfiture.

Turn up the path along the south fence of the churchyard (430196), cross the River Ash and climb steeply to turn right at the B1004 (432196) down The Holdens drive. Go right before a gate across the drive (431193 – footpath sign), down through trees to turn right through a kissing gate and left into a lane (429192). In 50 yards turn left by Two Bridges house over a stile, taking the left fork of the path to cross the river and bear right to cross a gravelled driveway (430191). Take the path down through the river meadows to turn left at a ford (430186) up a lane which bends right and left. In 20 yards, beyond this second bend, turn right on a bridleway along the bottom of a hornbeam wood for ⅓ mile, to where a bare hillside opens on the left. Turn left by a footbridge on your right (430179) and climb over the fields. Opposite three white houses with dark roofs turn right by a big oak tree (435179), then in 150 yards left by another, and follow the track to cross a stile in the corner of a hedge and walk down the driveway of Danetree House at Perry Green (439174), the headquarters of the Henry Moore Foundation.

Walking towards Perry Green you will see many Henry Moore sculptures in the fields and gardens around Danetree House and the nearby medieval Hoglands, Moore's home for more than 40 years until his death in 1986. A huge reclining figure on the skyline, enigmatic rounded and rectangular shapes, small totem-like pieces – they stand out of doors where Moore and his colleagues placed them. Many others, along with drawings and prints, are in storage. There are plans at the time of writing to build a study centre and a new gallery to display these works. By prior arrangement (see information box p. 80) you can view the collection before continuing with the walk.

Turn right at the road, and in 50 yards right opposite the Hoops Inn (footpath sign) along a stream edge and through fields to a road (434170). Go right here over the stream (footpath sign) and forward across two fields to the edge of a big gravelly rampart concealing a rubbish tip (432171); follow the rampart to the left, turn right through a gap and descend to a roadway that drops through trees. At the foot of the slope turn sharp right (427170) 50 yards before a weighbridge hut, and walk through the woods, rejoining the outward bridleway (430179) to regain the road (431184). Turn left to cross the ford and immediately right along a lane to a T-junction (429192), where you turn left to reach the High Street in Much Hadham opposite the Bull Inn.

Fifty yards along the street to the left stands Much Hadham forge (428191), a 16th-century building converted to a forge in 1811. This is a dark little beamed room, crammed with ironwork and tools, where the glowing hearth is still blown by hand with the original, much-patched leather bellows. You'll be welcome to watch the smith and his apprentices turning out gates, brackets, candlesticks and fire grates. Behind the forge is a little museum, well worth visiting.

From the forge walk up the High Street, admiring medieval cottages striped with timber beams and posts, oversailing upper storeys weighing down cramped ground-floor quarters, beautiful plasterwork on 16th- and 17th-century houses, a splendid red brick hall, all facing cobbled pavements – many lovely buildings to delight you on your way back to St Andrew's Church.

22

Bishop's Stortford to Harlow along the River Stort
(Herts/Essex border)

INFORMATION

Map OS 1:50,000 Landranger Sheet 167 'Chelmsford and Harlow'.

Travel

TRAIN (BR) – Bishop's Stortford.

CAR – M25 to Jct 27; M11 to Jct 8; A1250 to Bishop's Stortford. Park at station.

BUS – Green Line (Victoria) 081 668–7261. Local Information: 0923 257405. London Victoria–Bishop's Stortford: bus stops in Bridge Street, 5 mins from BR station (see map). Return Harlow (Cambridge Road, adjacent to Harlow Mill BR station)–London Victoria.

Length of walk 7 miles – linear – Bishop's Stortford station to Harlow Mill station (✄ *short cut* – 5 miles).

Conditions Riverside towpath – can be muddy after rain.

Refreshments Many pubs and cafés in Bishop's Stortford and Harlow.

This ramble through the peaceful, low-lying countryside of the Stort Valley connects Bishop's Stortford, one of the oldest towns in Hertfordshire, with Harlow New Town, one of the newest in Essex. Between the two runs the placid River Stort, winding its way past old mills and locks, under low ridges and through meadows rich in well-grown willows and alders.

Bishop's Stortford is a neat market town with a great pride in the appearance of its comfortable old red brick and half-timbered buildings. The town grew up around the ford where the Romans' Stone Street from Colchester to St Albans crossed the Stort. It's worth making a short detour up-river from the station to see the mound of Waytemore Castle, built by the Normans to defend a crook of the river and command the flat lands around. A Catholic prisoner in the castle in the reign of Queen Elizabeth I – one of many victims of religious bigotry

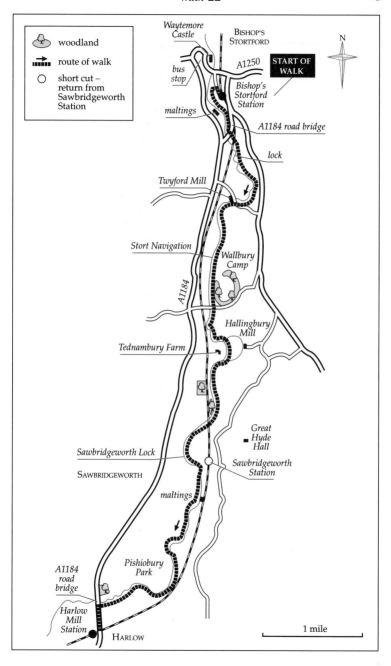

woodland

route of walk

short cut –
return from
Sawbridgeworth
Station

Waytemore Castle

Bishop's Stortford

A1250

START OF WALK

N

bus stop

Bishop's Stortford Station

maltings

A1184 road bridge

lock

Twyford Mill

Stort Navigation

Wallbury Camp

A1184

Hallingbury Mill

Tednambury Farm

Great Hyde Hall

Sawbridgeworth Lock

Sawbridgeworth Station

SAWBRIDGEWORTH

maltings

Pishiobury Park

A1184 road bridge

Harlow Mill Station

HARLOW

1 mile

incarcerated there over the centuries – described his quarters as 'nothing but a large vast room, cold water, bare walls, noe windows, but loopholes too highe to loke out at, nor bed nor bedstead . . .'

From Bishop's Stortford station (492209) turn right by the Falcon pub down Station Road to reach a bridge over the Stort by the Rose and Crown (490210). Walk down on the left of the bridge to the towpath, and follow it south for ⅓ mile to turn right along the A1184 (493204).

The old red brick maltings across the river just above the A1184 bridge, and the Tanners Arms beside the bridge, are reminders of the two trades that brought prosperity to Bishop's Stortford after the Quaker George Jackson turned the River Stort into the Stort Navigation in the 1760s. The opening ceremony in 1767 was a wild affair – townsfolk and canal navvies got so drunk that the beer supply had to be cut off. They were right to celebrate; the barges that took the malted barley and tanned leather to London made Bishop's Stortford's fortune.

From the A1184 bridge continue to follow the Stort, under a railway bridge and beside a weir, with a lock and its lock-keeper's cottage charmingly sited on a little islet (495199). Pass Twyford Mill (494193) to walk on below Wallbury Camp (493178).

Wallbury is an Iron Age hill fort covering more than 30 acres of a round hill. One local story says that this was where Julius Caesar accepted the surrender of the British tribes in 54 BC; another cites Wallbury as the burial place of that fierce Queen of the Iceni, Boudicca, at the bloody end of her uprising in 61 AD.

Below Tednambury Farm (491169) a looping short cut by the builders of the Stort Navigation isolated a crescent of ground, overlooked by the tall white bulk of Hallingbury Mill (496170). Cross the cut by footbridges and continue for a mile to reach Sawbridgeworth lock (486152) (✄ *short cut* – just beyond the lock is Sawbridgeworth station where you can catch a train back to Bishop's Stortford).

The lock carries a weight restriction notice placed there in 1930 by the Lee Conservancy, a canal company which had taken over the Stort Navigation 19 years before. The Stort was in such a sorry state by then that the Lee Conservancy was able to buy the whole concern for just five shillings.

There are splendid maltings all along the river through Sawbridgeworth – pagoda-topped roofs, bottle-shaped roasting kilns, tall chimneys, rows of windows and hundreds of yards of high, blank wall. But the subtle savour of roasting malt no longer wafts over the village.

These impressive old buildings house a mass of small industries these days.

Just across the river from the lock stands Great Hyde Hall (497155), seat of the Jocelyn family for many centuries. When Sir John Jocelyn died in 1741 his will stipulated that he should be buried in unconsecrated ground along with his best friend – his horse. Master and steed are sometimes seen, so they say, riding down the avenue to the Hall, inseparable in death as in life.

The towpath makes a long bend around the red brick pile of Pishiobury Park (480134) to run across meadows to the A1184 road bridge (471129) on the northern outskirts of Harlow. Turn left off the bridge above Harlow Mill to reach Harlow Mill station in ⅓ mile.

The little old medieval wool town of Harlow, and four satellite villages, were gobbled up by the great expansion begun in 1947 when the New Town was designated. Harlow New Town hangs like new washing from a line of road, river and railway, its sprawling modern estates smothering the once isolated villages of Great and Little Farndon, Latton and Netteswell.

23

Loughton to Epping
through Epping Forest
(Essex)

INFORMATION

Map OS 1:50,000 Landranger Sheet 167 'Chelmsford and
Harlow'.
Travel
   TUBE – Loughton (Central line).
   CAR – M25 to Jct 26; A121 to Loughton. Park at Loughton
   tube station.
Length of walk 7 miles – linear – Loughton tube station to
Epping tube station, returning by tube.
Conditions Woodland tracks, some parts churned up by horses.
Opening times *Epping Forest Centre, High Beach* Easter–end
October, Mondays–Saturdays 10–12.30, 2–5; Sundays and
public holidays 11–12.30, 2–5. 1 November–Easter, weekends
only, times as above.
Refreshments Holly Bush, Loughton (several other pubs); King's
Oak, High Beach; Spotted Dog, Ivy Chimneys.
Reading
   Booklets and leaflets available at Epping Forest Centre, High
   Beach (081 508–7714).
   Epping Forest by Sir William Addison (Robert Hale, 1977).

These woodland paths, especially enjoyable in the full blaze of autumn
colours, take a winding course through the length of Epping Forest.
There are wildly overgrown pollarded beeches and hornbeams to
admire in these lonely miles of forest, as well as two Iron Age forts
hidden away under the trees – one with memories of England's most
famous highwayman, Dick Turpin – and an excellent Forest Centre
half-way along the route.

**From Loughton station (423956) walk up the station approach
road and cross into Station Road; then cross the A121 (422962 –
the Holly Bush pub is to your left) into Forest Road, where the
trees of Epping Forest stand massed at the end of the road. Bear**

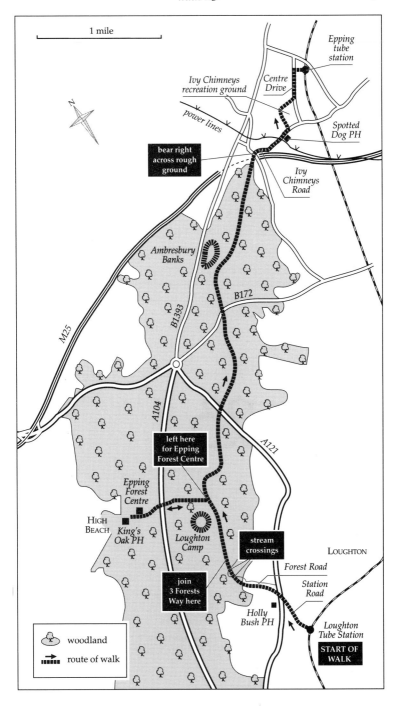

1 mile

Epping tube station

Ivy Chimneys recreation ground

Centre Drive

power lines

Spotted Dog PH

bear right across rough ground

Ivy Chimneys Road

Ambresbury Banks

B172

B1393

M25

A104

left here for Epping Forest Centre

A121

Epping Forest Centre

HIGH BEACH

King's Oak PH

Loughton Camp

stream crossings

LOUGHTON

Forest Road

Station Road

join 3 Forests Way here

Holly Bush PH

Loughton Tube Station

START OF WALK

woodland

route of walk

right onto the path through the forest (419965 – 'Hatfield Forest 22 miles ' sign) and walk beside the stream, crossing and then re-crossing it to bear left up the bank and right along the broad Three Forests Way bridleway (419969).

It's wonderfully peaceful under the great oak, beech and hornbeam trees that cover 6,000 acres of rolling Essex countryside. The forest was ten times that size in the 17th century when English monarchs ceased to hunt deer in their Royal Forest of Waltham, of which Epping Forest is the remnant. Local commoners had the right to graze their animals in the forest, and to pollard the trees and take the thinnings for fire-wood, building, tool handles and many other uses. But the forest was thoroughly abused over the centuries, as on Monken Hadley Common (see Walk No. 18) – poaching was rife, smallholders cleared huge areas illegally for farming and house-building, millions of trees were felled to build the navy's ships.

The 1878 Epping Forest Act of Parliament placed the forest under the control of the City of London Corporation, and it put a stop to all these encroachments, much to the fury of the commoners. New land was bought, the trees were properly managed and new areas planted. Epping Forest developed new problems as it became a popular place for outings from the East End – noise, litter, overcrowding with holiday-makers, a proliferation of cheapjack shows and stalls, the appearance of drunken parties of Londoners. By ever more thoughtful management these unpleasant manifestations disappeared, and now the forest is one of the most relaxing spots to stroll near London. One attractive side-effect of the curtailing of those Victorian commoners' rights is the sight of enormously overshot beech trees unpollarded for a century; from stubby trunks six feet high their pale grey branches shoot skywards 50 or 60 feet like giant tentacles.

Soon a grassy picnic space opens on your right; keep forward for 20 yards to turn left on a well-gravelled bridleway (421977).

On your left, smothered by trees, are the earthworks of the early Iron Age Loughton Camp (418975), dating from about 500 BC. The cele-brated highwayman Dick Turpin, a Whitechapel butcher's apprentice gone to the bad, had a hide-out in the 1730s in one of the pits that pockmark the centre of Loughton Camp. Along with other highway-men, Turpin used the fastnesses of Epping Forest as a base for cattle and horse thieving, which rapidly escalated into highway robbery. Eventually he fled to York, to be arrested in 1738 for the unglamorous felony of shooting a pheasant in the street, and was hanged for a long list of crimes on 7th April 1739. An unpleasant end – Turpin took five minutes to die.

Cross the A104 (415980) and follow a path to reach the Epping Forest Centre at High Beach (413981).

This is a well-run centre, opened in 1971, for exhibitions on forest life and nature, and for conservation courses. It's well worth spending half an hour enjoying the displays and learning about the great ecological value of Epping Forest, before walking across for a drink and snack at the King's Oak pub next door. There's a good view westward over wooded hills from the car park opposite.

Return to the bridleway at the picnic space, turn left and continue northwards; cross the A121 (429985) and in ⅓ mile turn left at a T-junction (NB white arrow on tree points *right* here) to cross the B172 (435995).

Soon you pass to the right of Ambresbury Banks (438003), another Iron Age fort covered in trees, the reputed site of Queen Boudicca's last stand during her rebellion against the Romans in the first century AD.

The path enters heathy country, to leave the trees (449010). Bear right across rough open land to a road, and cross into Ivy Chimneys Road. Go under power lines past the Spotted Dog pub, and in 100 yards turn left (456010 – footpath sign) up Ivy Chimneys recreation ground and over a stile. Bear right to a road in a housing estate; turn left along it, then left up Centre Drive (458013). In 250 yards turn right opposite No. 77 along a narrow alleyway to reach Epping station and your tube back to Loughton.

24

Debden, Lambourne
and Theydon Bois
(Essex)

INFORMATION

Map OS 1:50,000 Landranger Sheet 167 'Chelmsford and
  Harlow'.
Travel
  TUBE – Debden (Central line).
  CAR – M25 to Jct 26; A121 to Loughton; A1168 to Debden
    tube station. Park at station.
Length of walk 6½ miles – linear – Debden tube station to
  Theydon Bois tube station; return by tube.
Conditions Field paths and country roads.
Refreshments White Hart or Blue Boar, Abridge; Bull or Railway
  Arms, Theydon Bois.
Reading Booklet available in St Mary's Church, Lambourne.

Wide views over the countryside of west Essex, a remarkable Norman
church beautified in Georgian times and a stroll beside the River
Roding – these are the pleasures of this walk in the triangle of rural
country between the M25 and M11.

**Turn right out of Debden station (442961), skirt the station build-
ing and cross the railway line by the footbridge to turn left along
a pathway between wire fences. Emerging by the Bank of England's
printing works, turn right and immediately left down a pathway to
turn left along a footpath in front of the printing works (446960).
The path runs into fields at a stile; follow waymark arrows around
hornbeam woods to cross the M11 over a footbridge (455970). The
track snakes across fields to Piggott's Farm and the B172 (465971);
cross to the pavement and turn right into Abridge over the bridge.**

Abridge was once 'Aeffa's bridge', and the village developed around the
crossing of the river between Romford and Epping. There's a fine view
of old buildings and willow trees bordering the river from the Georgian
bridge that spans the Roding today. Whether Abridge still merits the

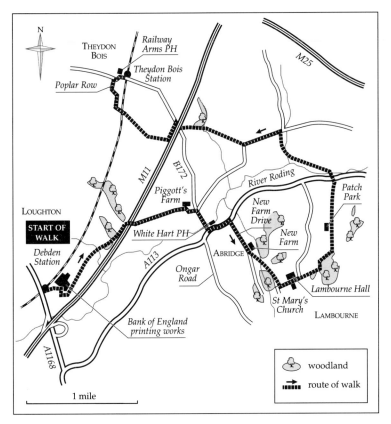

name of 'the little Sodom' that it earned in the 19th century through the wild behaviour of its inhabitants, you'll have to decide for yourself.

Turn left along Ongar Road, and in 400 yards go right up New Farm Drive (470970). Just past New Farm (472966) a stile on the left leads into a field. Follow waymarks (little green arrows inside yellow ones) over fields and into a wood (475963); in 250 yards go left across a footbridge and stile, following the pathway to the right to a trackway where you turn left for Lambourne church (479961).

St Mary's Church is unique – a Norman church strikingly restored in the 1720s. There is nothing about the exterior, with its typical Essex weatherboarded tower, diminutive steeple and early Norman north and south doorways, to prepare you for the splendours of Georgian plasterwork inside. The king post of the nave roof sprouts fantastic acanthus leaves; the chancel arch is flattened and encrusted with plaster foliage; the roof beams are sheathed in yet more highly decorated plasterwork. The sturdy wooden gallery at the west end is inscribed with details of benefactions and the legend 'This Gallery was built at the Charge of William Walker, Citizen and Ironmonger of London 1704'. The south wall of the nave carries a 14th-century wall painting of St Christopher, gazing sideways in mild-mannered wonder at the Holy Child on his shoulder. In the south windows of the chancel are exquisitely painted 17th-century panels of Swiss glass, featuring biblical figures with the impassive faces and contemporary costume of Swiss burghers of the 1630s.

It's worth lingering long over the elaborate wall monuments to the Lockwood family of Lambourne Hall, which tell of mighty deeds of arms and of the tranquil lives of country gentry. A gloriously-robed angel with a trumpet tops the memorial to Captain George Lockwood of the 8th Hussars, who was killed during the Charge of the Light Brigade; while fulsome praises commemorate Catherine Lockwood (died 1743 – 'remarkably chearful . . . a natural charming Temper, Accomplish'd Behaviour and good Understanding') and her husband Richard, a member of Parliament until 'Thinking himself incapable of doing his Country any Farther Publick Service, He retir'd from the Fatigues of Busyness'.

Continue along the lane from the church, keeping straight on in 150 yards ('Abridge Country Walk' sign and green-within-yellow arrow waymark) to bear left around the edge of a wood. Skirt the wood to join a grassy path leading due north to pass through the farmyard of Patch Park (485969). Cross the A113 (485976) and a footbridge over the River Roding, and turn left along its bank.

This meandering stretch of the Roding, famous among fishermen for its big chub, slips under willows, its rushes loud with squawking moorhens. Wooded ridges make a far-flung frame for the broad, flat river valley, out of which lines of poplars rise darkly.

Follow the river for ⅓ mile to cross a tributary stream by a foot-bridge (478979) and follow a fence on your left to a road. Turn left for 400 yards, then at a sharp left-hand bend go right over a stile (472981). Cross two fields diagonally over stiles, and keep to the left edge of the third field all the way up to the M11 (463983). Go under the motorway and turn immediately left over a stile, to follow green-within-yellow arrows for a mile over fields to cross the railway on the outskirts of Theydon Bois (454985). Bear right through a housing estate to reach a T-junction with Poplar Row (453989) opposite the enormous village green.

Turn right along Poplar Row to cross the main B172 road (454990) and follow Theydon Bois station signs to the station and your train back to Debden.

Theydon Bois is strung loosely around its wide green heart, a mixture of modern houses, old cottages and pubs that are easy on the eye. The wood after which the Normans named the village – an outlying section of Epping Forest – still stands, though encroached on by recent development. Theydon Bois was a small rural village until the tube trains arrived and allowed London commuters to live out here in green and pleasant Essex.

25

North Weald and Greensted Church
(Essex)

INFORMATION

Map OS 1:50,000 Landranger Sheet 167 'Chelmsford and Harlow'.

Travel

  Tube – North Weald (Central line) Open peak times (train info – tel 071 222-1234) Monday – Friday at time of writing, but under threat of closure mid-1993.

  Car – M25 to Jct 27; M11 north to Jct 7; A414 towards Chipping Ongar; in 3 miles, B181 to North Weald Bassett. Park at North Weald tube station.

Length of walk 9½ miles – circular – start and finish at North Weald tube station (✂ *short cut* – 6 ½ miles).

Conditions Field paths and country roads. Take care walking on roads – many sharp bends.

Refreshments Drill House (532025 – between Toot Hill and Greensted).

Reading Booklets available in churches at Stanford Rivers and Greensted.

Explore the two notable churches at Stanford Rivers and Greensted, and saunter along the bridleways and footpaths of this well-wooded corner of west Essex. Greensted's little Church of St Andrew is the oldest wooden church in the world, a memorable focal point of this walk in quiet country.

From North Weald station (497036) turn right in 15 yards along a path that crosses the railway and climbs to Cold Hall Farm (500033).

At the time of writing you can look back from this high point to see – if your timing is right – the Central line's little red train clacking along through the rural Essex fields: a strange sight and sound, a snippet of familiar London life far from its usual setting, soon to disappear if

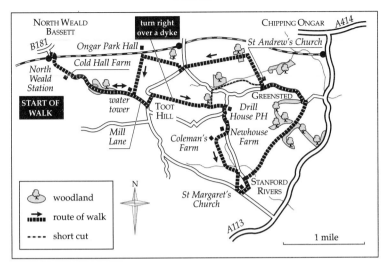

closure is carried out. But a private company has plans to replace it with a steam train – even better to see and hear.

From Cold Hall Farm bend left along the bridleway, then in 200 yards go right (502032) to pass through a wood and continue, to meet Mill Lane by a water tower (512029). At the road at Toot Hill (516026) turn left, then keep ahead at a sharp left-hand bend (517028 – 'Essex Way' sign) into a field. Turn right along the hedge and in 250 yards, at the foot of the slope, go right between an oak and an ash to cross a dyke and a stile – then keep the hedge on your left and continue over the fields for a mile to a road by the Drill House pub (532025) (✂ *short cut* – 300 yards before the Drill House, take a footpath on the left just beyond a ruined farmhouse to cross a road and rejoin the walk at St Andrew's Church in Greensted).

The pub sign shows a dappled horse pulling an old-fashioned seed drill, but the reality behind the name is less amiable. 18th-century young offenders were given a military drilling in fields near here in the original 'short sharp shock' treatment.

Turn right and keep ahead at the road bend ('Stanford Rivers' sign) to pass Newhouse Farm (531021). In 150 yards go right over a stile and follow the marked footpath to Coleman's Farm (529019).

These two farmhouses with their steep, red-tiled roofs, tall chimneys and white gables blend perfectly with their landscape. The modern building in front of Coleman's Farm, trying to copy the style, shows how much sympathy our present-day architects have lost with the surroundings in which they work. Is it the use of purely local materials that gives the two farmhouses such harmonious qualities, or just the dignity and simplicity of old age?

In front of Coleman's Farm a bridleway sign points to the left down a sunken lane that meets a tarred road (532013). Just before a T-junction with another road turn right and up a field edge to St Margaret's Church at Stanford Rivers (534009).

St Margaret's has the typical Essex weatherboarded tower and little spire, and a richly carved 14th-century north porch. Inside, the Norman nave is big and barn-like, with a solid black wood gallery at the west end. On each side of the altar are fine brasses in the floor – on the north side to Thomas Greville, wrapped in his christening robe, a 'chrisom child' who died in 1492 less than a month after his birth; and on the south Robert Borrow, a long-haired Tudor knight in great round-toed 'sollerets' or iron shoes. Under the gallery is a modern painting of the Nativity, with soft light shining from the infant Jesus on the faces of angels and onlookers.

From the church gate walk left and left again ('Greensted; Ongar' sign); ignore the first track on the right and take the second (535011) for 1½ miles through the fields to a road (548025). Turn left (take care – successive bends!) and walk ½ mile to Greensted Church (539030) (✇ *short cut* – rejoins here).

St Andrew's Church at Greensted is a famous building – the oldest wooden church in the world. The great oak trunks, split in half, that form the walls of the nave have been dated back to 845 AD. Legend says that the body of St Edmund, martyred by the Danes in 870 AD, rested here for a night in 1013 on its journey to Bury St Edmunds from London. In the dark, ship-like interior hangs a painting of about 1500 AD of the blissfully smiling saint tied to a tree, stuck with arrows, while grim-faced archers bend their bows and a wolf guards the saint's severed head. The wooden nave is flanked by a 17th-century weatherboarded tower and a Tudor brick chancel – three entirely disparate elements that somehow blend beautifully.

Pass the church tower and walk north through the farmyard of Hall Farm (concrete footpath sign and green-within-yellow arrow way-mark) on a track that rises to meet a green lane in woodland (535036 – 'Greensted country walk' finger post). Turn left for ½ mile to reach tarmac at Pensons Lane (528035) and walk forward to go over a crossroads (524033 – 'Toot Hill and Epping' sign). In 150 yards turn right opposite Hardings Farm (concrete footpath sign) up a field edge. In 75 yards, where the path bends right by a garden, turn left across the field (522033), aiming for a telegraph pole on its own, 50 yards out from its neighbour at the edge of a

wood. From the pole aim straight ahead between two oaks towards a cluster of radio masts. Go through the hedge at the bottom of the field (wooden post with yellow arrow) and keep the same line ahead to meet a farm trackway by a bridge under the tube line (513036), where you turn left. The track rises for ¾ mile to meet your outward path ¼ mile west of Toot Hill (512029); turn right here to return to North Weald station.

Havering-atte-Bower
and Stapleford Abbotts
(Essex)

INFORMATION

Map OS 1:50,000 Landranger Sheet 177 'East London'.

Travel

  CAR – M25 to Jct 28; A12 towards London; at Gallows
    Corner (2 miles), last exit on right; 2½ miles to Havering-
    atte-Bower. Park by village green.

  BUS – Green Line (Victoria) 081 668–7261. Local informa-
    tion: 0245 492211 (ext. 51587/51594). BR from Liverpool
    Street or LT red bus 86 from Stratford to Romford; 500,
    501, 502 to Havering-atte-Bower village green.

Length of walk 6 miles – circular – start and finish at Havering-
    atte-Bower village green.

Conditions Field paths, lanes and roads. Some paths overgrown,
    and a missing footbridge at 511954 – careful attention to
    map and instructions necessary.

Church key St Mary's, Stapleford Abbotts – key from Old
    Rectory Farm across lane.

Refreshments Orange Tree or The Willows, Havering-atte-
    Bower; Royal Oak, Nuper's Hatch.

Reading Church and village notes in St John's Church,
    Havering-atte-Bower.

This challenging walk leads you from the ridge-top village of Havering-
atte-Bower, where English monarchs once had their royal manor, across
rolling Essex farmland to the Victorian church at Stapleford Abbotts,
notorious for being condemned as 'hideous' by Sir Nikolaus Pevsner.
The return route leads down into the pleasant depths of the valley of
the River Rom, before climbing again to a good view of Havering-atte-
Bower on the skyline.

Havering-atte-Bower's big rectangular village green lies spread like
a tablecloth before the handsome Victorian church of St John the
Evangelist, a large flint-walled building finished in 1878 and unusually

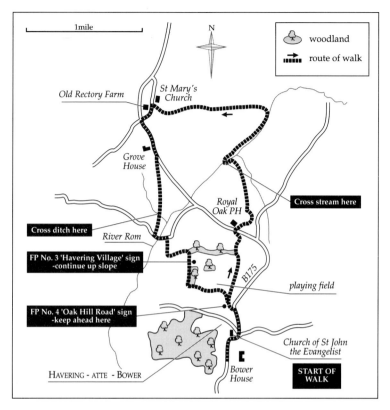

attractive for a high Victorian church. Behind the altar is a painting of the Last Supper, with lively apostles' faces and a glowering Judas Iscariot sulking over his moneybag. The wall memorial to Collinson and Cecilia Hall is my favourite. Mr Hall poses uncomfortably in a stiff collar, flanked by a wench holding a sickle and crowned with ears of corn – her expression is definitely more fed-up than sorrowful. In a relief panel below, a traction engine belches steam as it chuffs between stooks of corn.

The old village stocks stand on the corner of the green, where on the site of the church once stood a royal manor used by English monarchs from Edward the Confessor to Charles I, a handy base for hunting expeditions in nearby Hainault Forest. In the early 19th century a hut on the green was home to Elizabeth Balls and her 50 goats: a 'disappointment in her affections' drove this mild-mannered woman to take up her hermit's life.

A few hundred yards down the B175 towards Romford stands Bower House, a fine red brick house built in 1729 by John Baynes, partly of materials salvaged from the ruins of the royal manor. The ghost of his daughter, Lucy, haunts the place.

From the church (512930) turn left along the village street, and left again in 300 yards (512934 – 'FP No. 3 Bournebridge' sign) down a tarred track that bends right. Keep ahead at 'FP No. 4 Oak Hill Road' sign, skirting a playing field to walk through fields and a neck of woodland, following yellow arrow waymarks, to the B175 (512943). Cross between a garage and the Royal Oak; at the far left -hand corner of the pub car park a 'FP Nupers Hatch' sign points along an overgrown path beside garden fences which reaches a lane (513947).

Turn left to pass Nupers Farm and at the end of the track keep forward (512950) over a field and through a hedge to the stream in the bottom corner. Walk left here, looking for a crossing point. A fallen willow 150 yards to the left of the field corner makes a handy span over which to scramble.

This part of the walk is used so little that the footbridge at 511954 is gone. You'll probably have found the path beyond the Royal Oak a brambly and nettly stretch, too. This is where country walking gets its savour – a touch of adventure, even in this well-tamed land-scape.

Once across the stream, turn left and follow it to a lane (516960); turn left to the end of the lane and keep straight forward for a mile over stiles and across fields, keeping hedges, strips of woodland and field banks on your right till you reach St Mary's Church at Stapleford Abbotts (501961).

Pevsner must have been having a bad day when he condemned St Mary's as 'hideous'. The brick tower, built in the year of Waterloo, and the crazy-paved nave of 1862 don't blend well, but the porch is richly carved and the plain interior harmonious. The Great War memorial has a nice coloured enamel picture of St George and the Dragon, and in the north chapel is a relief memorial portrait of Sir John Abdy supported by a grief-stricken cherub. The simple brick Abdy Chapel at the back of the church was built in 1638.

Retrace your steps for 50 yards from the church and turn right over a stile to reach the B175, where you cross and turn left for 400 yards. Just past Grove House go right over a stile (501955) and cross a field to a farm track, which runs down into the wide and lovely valley of the River Rom. Cross a ditch to the right at the bottom (501946) and bear right to the road (501943). Turn left, ignoring a footpath sign opposite, cross the river and in 150 yards go right (502943) to cross a stile and a field. Over another stile turn left round the edge of a big field; woodland joins on your left (505940 – 'FP No. 3 Havering Village' sign). Keep ahead up the slope to bear left around the corner of the wood (505937) and keep a hedge on your left (good view of Havering-atte-Bower straddling the crest of the ridge across the valley) to reach the playing field (510937). Turn right here (FP yellow arrow) and make for the tower of St John's Church.

27

Laindon Common
and Little Burstead
(Essex)

INFORMATION

Map OS 1:50,000 Landranger Sheet 177 'East London'.
Travel
> CAR – M25 to Jct 29; A127 towards Southend; A176 towards Billericay; in 2½ miles turn left just before roundabout; car park on left in 100 yards.
> BUS – Green Line (Victoria) 081 668–7261. Local information: 0245 492211 (ext. 51587/51594). London Victoria–Basildon–Laindon Common; bus stops on A176 Billericay Road, 50 yards before Laindon Common turning (see map).

Length of walk 4 miles – circular – start and finish at car park on Laindon Common.
Conditions Woodland, field and common land paths. Wiggins Lane can be muddy.
Refreshments Duke's Head, Laindon Common.
Reading 'Little Burstead Circular Walk' (Walk No. 3) in Basildon Council's *Greenway Countryside Walks* booklet (tel: 0268 550088/559833).

Rough old Essex commons still survive in the triangle of gently rolling farming countryside between built-up Basildon, Brentwood and Billericay, and a network of old lanes threads them. The dark pond where the River Crouch has its beginning and the hump-backed church of St Mary the Virgin at Little Burstead are two focal points on this walk.

From the car park (674930), cross the road and turn left in front of Stockwell House to pass Frith Cottage and continue across Laindon Common (Basildon District Circular Footpath green arrow waymarker).

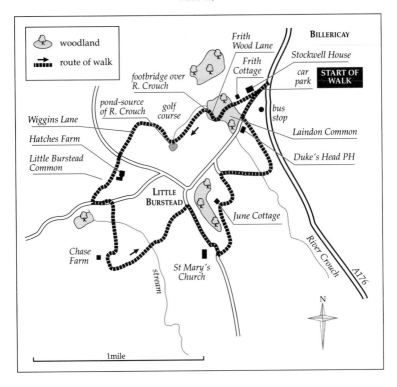

woodland

route of walk

Frith Wood Lane

BILLERICAY

Frith Cottage

Stockwell House

footbridge over R. Crouch

car park

START OF WALK

pond-source of R. Crouch

golf course

bus stop

Wiggins Lane

Laindon Common

Hatches Farm

Little Burstead Common

LITTLE BURSTEAD

Duke's Head PH

June Cottage

Chase Farm

stream

St Mary's Church

River Crouch

A176

N

1mile

This part of Laindon Common has escaped building – so far – and remains much as it was: gorse and birch scrub, bushy oaks, copses of silver birch and aspen on damp ground – a jungle where birds sing and rabbits scurry.

At the end of the path keep ahead past a wooden horse barrier and on through a wood, to turn right up Frith Wood Lane (670929) and in 150 yards left across the infant River Crouch, continuing up a hedge that bisects a golf course.

Try dating this hedge by the long-established rule-of-thumb method: every species of woody tree in a measured 30 yards represents 100 years. I spotted oak, elder, hawthorn, sloe, hazel, hornbeam, ash and aspen – perhaps 800 years old?

The pond at the end of the hedge (665925) is the source of the River Crouch, which winds away eastwards for 25 miles to broaden into a wide-mouthed estuary. The pond gleams darkly among large yews, swollen oaks, willows and a few wild service trees with their long-fingered, toothed leaves – sure indicators of ancient woodland.

Bear right over a stile under a big field maple beside the pond, then left to follow a chalky path across a golf course. This area was once known as The Wilderness – a name to bring a wry smile as you survey the shaven, manicured acres of fairways. At a stile (662928 – red arrows) turn left into Wiggins Lane.

Wiggins Lane was once a busy road; you could still fit a dual carriageway between its tall hedges, but the undergrowth has crept inwards to leave only a strip of trackway in the middle. These hedges make another good challenge for rough-and-ready dating: Wiggins Lane might well date back to Norman times.

Cross a road (660924) into Hatches Farm Road to pass the handsome old Tudor farmhouse, bearing right off the road at the next left-hand bend (659922) to follow a path down across the bushy wastes of Little Burstead Common. Turn left along the road (658920) and in 200 yards right (FP 54 sign) across a valley, rising to a grassy mound to the left of Chase Farm. Turn left here (660915) down a broad field track into the valley bottom, with the spire of Little Burstead church on its hilltop ahead. Cross the stream and bear diagonally left up the field slope to follow the crest of the ridge to the road (667920), where you turn right for the church (669915).

On to the Norman nave of St Mary's, the Tudor builders tacked a chancel with fine brick window frames. The 15th-century wooden belfry with its broach spire stands proudly above the trees, marking the isolated church in the landscape for miles around. Angels hold up the medieval roof timbers. St Mary's is a lonely delight.

At the top of the church path, cross the road, turn right and in 50 yards left ('FP 50 Great Burstead' sign) to bear right along a hedge. At the field corner go right through the hedge and over a footbridge; then turn left (671916) to cross two fields to a lane (670920). Turn right and follow the lane round to the left, bearing right in 200 yards by June Cottage (670923). Keep ahead through trees to cross the River Crouch (673923) and walk up a field slope, turning left in front of a stile to cross the tops of three fields and go through a thicket to reach the Duke's Head pub (672928). Turn right here through the trees beside the road to reach the car park.

28

Thrift Wood
and Charity Lane
(Essex)

INFORMATION

Map OS 1:50,000 Landranger Sheets 167 'Chelmsford and
Harlow' and 168 'Colchester and The Blackwater'.

Travel CAR – M25 to Jct 28; A12 to Chelmsford bypass; A414
towards Maldon; in Danbury village turn right at 'Bicknacre'
sign (774053) on minor road for 2 miles; bear right on
B1418 through Bicknacre village. Park at Brewers Arms on
the right.

Length of walk 6 miles – circular – start and finish at Brewers
Arms.

Conditions Woodland and field paths, country roads. Woodland
paths often very muddy. Take tree identification book.

Refreshments Brewers Arms, Bicknacre.

Reading *Thrift Wood* Wildside Walk leaflet from Essex County
Council Planning Department, County Hall, Chelmsford,
Essex.

This walk in an unfrequented part of rural Essex is all about green lanes
and green woods. The green lanes meander between ancient farmsteads
well away from any main road, while the woodlands stand as remnants
of the original wildwood that once covered England – one of them,
Thrift Wood, is managed as a coppice in the traditional way by the
Essex Wildlife Trust.

**From the Brewers Arms (788021) cross the B1418, turn right, and
in 10 yards left into a bridleway (fingerpost), which reaches a crossroads of tracks in 300 yards (790022). Continue straight over this,
then 10 yards further on bear right, and in another 50 yards right
again over a stile into Thrift Wood. Keep ahead for ¼ mile on a
winding path to reach a clearing (791017).**

The smooth, slender multiple stems of hornbeams stand each side of the
path, their tooth-edged leaves filtering the sunlight. Sweet chestnuts,

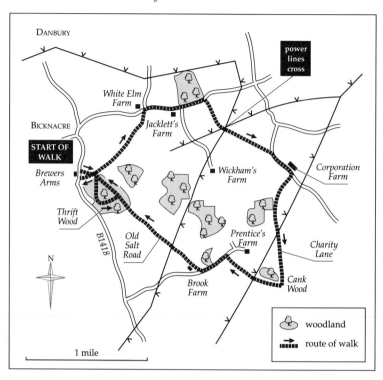

with their long, sharply-toothed leaves, form clumps among the horn-beams under the tall oak standards that were planted as protective 'big brothers' for the coppice trees. In the clearing you'll probably find cut and stacked boughs of hornbeam, piles of sawn logs and the ashes of fires – not sylvan vandalism, but careful management of this long-neglected and now productive wood by the Essex Wildlife Trust.

Apart from the many uses of the cut wood, coppicing (cutting the shoots growing from the ancient 'stools' or stumps of hornbeam and sweet chestnut) has opened up areas of Thrift Wood to sun and rain, allowing wild flowers to grow. One of these plants, common cow-wheat (pale yellow two-lipped flowers with orange 'tongues' between the petal lips), is the food plant of the rare heath fritillary butterfly, which declined to extinction in Essex as the traditional coppice woodlands ceased to be managed. But the heath fritillaries of Thrift Wood, re-introduced here by the Trust in 1984 to feed on the newly resurgent common cow-wheat, are thriving.

Bear left on entering the clearing ('Wildside Walk' sign) to reach the edge of Thrift Wood and turn left (794019) to return to the junction of tracks at 790022, at the *second* of two fingerposts. From here bear diagonally right between hedges across fields for

½ mile on an old green drove road to reach the B1418 at White Elm Farm (797029), where the body of a highwayman lies buried at the crossroads with a stake of elm driven through his heart. Turn right along a minor road past the medieval farmstead of Jacklett's Farm (800030).

Jacklett's, and the moated Wickham's Farm half a mile south, have been farmsteads since at least Plantagenet times. Their names recall yeomen of the Middle Ages – Roger Joket and John de Wycoumbe, who farmed these lands in the 14th century.

A quarter of a mile beyond Jacklett's Farm, turn right over a stile on a path that goes under a junction of power lines (808028) to meet a road on a bend (813024). Turn right for ¼ mile, then right again opposite Corporation Farm (816022 – fingerpost) into Charity Lane.

Charity Lane leads south to Charity Farm, which once generated the money to educate local children. This is a delightful green lane running straight and true between thick old hedges – oak, ash, holly, hornbeam, hawthorn, elm, blackthorn – a lane rich in birdsong and butterflies, perhaps as old as those medieval farmsteads nearby.

After a mile turn right around the corner of Cank Wood (815008) and follow the path to turn left (808011) along the drive from Prentice's Farm. At the road bend go right (805009 – fingerpost) past Brook Farm along the Old Salt Road. Continue along the Old Salt Road for a mile, to pass the edge of Thrift Wood and return to the Brewer's Arms.

Another green lane and another story. Salt panned and packed on the banks of the River Crouch to the south was carried to Chelmsford in the Middle Ages – perhaps long before – along this now forgotten highway through the heart of Essex.

29

Bradwell and
St Peter's-on-the-Wall
(Essex)

INFORMATION

Map OS 1:50,000 Landranger Sheet 168 'Colchester and The
   Blackwater'.
Travel CAR – M25 to Jct 28; A12 to Chelmsford bypass; A414
   to Maldon; B1018 and B1010 to Latchingdon; on sharp
   right-hand bend by church, keep ahead on minor road
   through Mayland and Steeple for 8 miles, to bear left on
   B1021 and reach Bradwell Waterside. Park at marina.
Length of walk 6½ miles – circular – start and finish at the
   Green Man pub, Bradwell Waterside.
Conditions Sea wall path and country roads. Bring binoculars.
Refreshments Green Man, Bradwell Waterside; King's Head,
   Bradwell-on-Sea.
Reading
   Booklets on St Peter's Chapel and the Roman fort of Othona
      on sale in St Peter's Chapel and in St Thomas's Church,
      Bradwell-on-Sea.
   Bradwell Cockle Spit Wildside Walk leaflet from Essex
      County Council Planning Department, County Hall,
      Chelmsford, Essex.

Only the Isle of Sheppey walk (No. 34) can vie with this one for
remoteness. Here is a real taste of lonely Essex marshland, out on the
northernmost tip of the unfrequented Dengie peninsula. Here you are
guaranteed solitude, salt wind in your hair and thousands of sea birds
for company (waders in summer, geese in winter). At the most isolated
corner of the walk you reach the oldest Saxon chapel still in use in
Britain, the unique and atmospheric St Peter's-on-the-Wall.

**From the Green Man pub (994078) turn right along the sea wall
path to pass Bradwell nuclear power station (001090) and continue
round the tip of the peninsula for 3½ miles.**

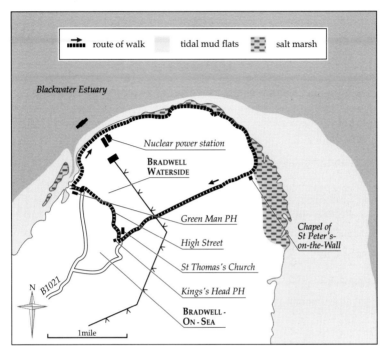

| route of walk | tidal mud flats | salt marsh |

Blackwater Estuary

Nuclear power station

BRADWELL WATERSIDE

Green Man PH

High Street

St Thomas's Church

King's's Head PH

BRADWELL - ON - SEA

Chapel of St Peter's- on-the-Wall

N B1021

1mile

To your left you look out over the muddy tides of the Blackwater estuary towards low-lying, remote marshes more than a mile away across the water. On your right are the flat fields of the Dengie peninsula, their horizontals broken by isolated trees and farms. There's nowhere quite like Dengie for loneliness, even in these days of easy travel. A hundred years ago this was prime smuggling country, a foreign land to Londoners. Dengie folk had a reputation for surliness, ignorance and savage behaviour with their fists and with their liquor – not undeserved.

In summer the salt marshes below the sea wall are hazed with the delicate purple of sea lavender, and the mud flats beyond them ring with curlew and oystercatcher cries. But it's worth braving Dengie's biting east winds in late autumn and winter as well, when packs of dark-bellied brent geese from Siberia bark like hounds in the sky and flock to the tideline to feed on eel-grass, while visiting knot, sanderling, dunlin and grey plover pick over the mud with their long, probing bills.

The sea wall path turns south round the blunt tip of the peninsula., to reach the lonely chapel of St Peter's-on-the-Wall (031081).

St Peter's has a special atmosphere, unlike any other church – partly due to its wonderfully remote position, partly to its great age. It has stood out here facing the marshes for well over 1300 years. St Cedd, a Celtic bishop trained on Holy Island in Northumberland, brought the Word south to the Godforsaken folk of Essex in 654 AD, and built the church much as it stands today. The saint used the materials that lay to hand – the stones and thin red tiles of the Roman shore fort of Othona, above whose gateway he founded St Peter's. There are tall, narrow Saxon windows and arches in the church, along with signs of more recent and less godly alterations – notably a big area of roughly mended stone-work in the north and south walls where farmers smashed holes to let their hay-wagons in when St Peter's was doing duty as a barn. Today, however, the church is used for occasional services once more – a truly extraordinary continuity thirteen centuries long.

From the chapel, walk west for two miles down the road, to reach St Thomas's Church in Bradwell-on-Sea (004069).

These days the village lies a mile inland, in spite of its name – evidence of the steady reclamation of marshland for agriculture in times past. The 14th-century church of St Thomas stands in the crook of the road, beautifully looked after inside and out, with the old village felon's cage in the south-east corner of the churchyard. Beside the gate stands a mounting block for horseback parishioners, its steps hollowed by centuries of riding boots.

Turn right up High Street for ½ mile, and where it bends left into Trusses Road (002075) take the footpath in the angle of the roads which leads across fields to Bradwell Waterside and the Green Man pub.

The Green Man is a marvellous pub – panelled in dark wood, cool and shady, floored with stone flags, a place for good conversation. Eighteenth-century Bradwell smugglers used the Green Man's many nooks and crannies to hide their barrels and bales of contraband from the excise men.

See if you can decipher the enigmatic notice that hangs above the old kitchen range in the bar.

30

Around the sea walls
of Canvey Island
(Essex)

INFORMATION

Map OS 1:50,000 Landranger Sheet 178 'The Thames Estuary'.
Travel
   TRAIN (BR) – Benfleet.
   CAR – M25 to Jct 30; A13 towards Southend-on-Sea; right on
      A130 at South Benfleet on to Canvey Island; at round-
      about turn left on B1014 for a mile to Benfleet station.
      Park near station.
   BUS – Green Line (Victoria) 081 668–7261. Local
      Information: 0245 492211 (ext. 51587/51594). London
      Victoria–Tarpots Corner–Benfleet BR station.
Length of walk 14 miles – circular – start and finish at Benfleet
   station
Conditions Sea wall path, well surfaced.
Refreshments The Lobster Smack Inn, Canvey Village.
Reading
   Canvey Island – The History of a Marshland Community by
      Basil E. Cracknell (available in Canvey Island's public
      library).
   The Other British Isles by Christopher Somerville (Grafton
      Books 1990) – see Chapter 2.
   Listening Many evocative recordings by Dr Feelgood –
      information from Grand Records, 107a High Street,
      Canvey Island, Essex SS8 7RF.

All right – I admit it! Canvey Island is just about the last place most walkers would dream of venturing for a long day's ramble. Set in a bleak angle of the Thames estuary, half-full of ramshackle shops and night spots, caravans and less-than-opulent housing, laden with oil and gas storage cylinders, Canvey Island has nothing in common with the peaceful rural walks that fill this book. But have faith! There's a lot more to Canvey than its uncompromising reputation would have you believe . . .

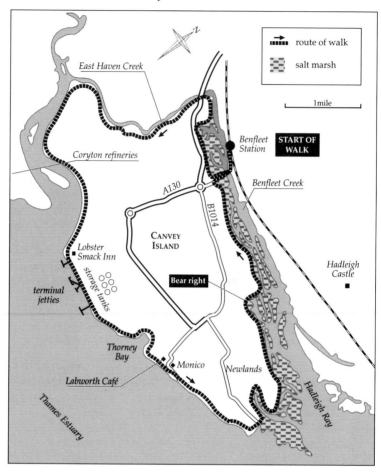

route of walk

salt marsh

1 mile

East Haven Creek

Coryton refineries

A130

B1014

Benfleet Station

START OF WALK

Benfleet Creek

CANVEY ISLAND

Lobster Smack Inn

storage tanks

terminal jetties

Bear right

Hadleigh Castle

Thorney Bay

Monico

Newlands

Labworth Café

Thames Estuary

Hadleigh Ray

From Benfleet station (778859) turn left along the B1014 to cross the bridge over Benfleet Creek (780856). Turn immediately right through a gate and across a plank footbridge, then left to reach the sea wall (779853), where you turn right along the path.

Canvey Island looks dead flat, and it is – the whole island lies below spring tide levels, protected from the Thames floodwaters by the sea wall you are walking. A Dutchman, Joos Croppenburgh, built the first wall around Canvey in 1620 – before then there were six islands here, good sheep-grazing ground covered with water at each spring tide. The green meadows around you look much the same as they did then - which can't be said for most of Canvey.

In a mile you cross the A130 bridge (765861) and continue along the sea wall beside East Benfleet Creek in a flat green landscape,

**lonely and windswept, for two miles to reach an ancient wooden
jetty opposite the Shell Haven refineries (750839).**

Only the muddy width of the creek separates Canvey Island from the
huge complex of oil refineries, their chimneys flaring against the sky,
and the white cylinders of oil and gas storage tanks at Shell Haven. This
is where Canvey's other face begins to show – a grimly fascinating one.

In another two miles you reach the Lobster Smack (772822), an old
weatherboarded smugglers' pub, Charles Dickens's 'Ship Inn' in *Great
Expectations*, where Pip hid the convict Magwitch to wait for escape on
a continental steamer. On the river side of the sea wall is a tangled
geometry of jetties, where oil and gas tankers unload their cargo into
pipelines and the big storage silos further along the wall – an impressive sight as the giant ships loom massively at their moorings.

**Continue past the jetties and storage tanks, round the large cara-
van park in Thorney Bay (795825) and on past the circular art
deco Labworth Café on the sea wall (801824) to arrive opposite the
shabby old Monico nightspot (802825).**

When the bridge over Benfleet Creek was built in 1931, London's East
Enders rushed down to remote Canvey Island; some to build houses,
others for a weekend's raucous fun. This eastern half of the island is
chock-full of houses, cranky little shops and dubious clubs and dance
halls. This is the world of Dr Feelgood, Canvey Island's celebrated
rhythm 'n' blues band, whose wild playing and hard-edged lyrics have
celebrated this close-knit, tough place for 20 years. Dr Feelgood's office
is still where it always was, above a bookie's in Canvey's High Street,
and the band is still touting its Canvey toughness all over the world.

**The sea wall path continues, to turn inland at the eastern end of
Canvey Island (822830). Bear left (822834), then right round the
creek that shelters the boats of Canvey's yacht club (816835), to
turn west along the northern edge of the island.**

Here yet another of Canvey's many faces greets you – the wide marshes
and mud flats of Hadleigh Ray, overlooked on the mainland shore by
the ruined towers of medieval Hadleigh Castle; a quiet stretch of lonely
marshland full of bird cries. On the night of 31st January 1953 the
catastrophic East Coast flood disaster fell on Canvey at this spot, when
an abnormal sea surge driven by high winds broke through the sea wall
above Newlands (805844) and poured over the island, drowning
58 people in a few minutes.

**Beyond Newlands bear right (801845) with the sea wall – a newly
strengthened one – and walk on for another 1½ miles to reach the
B1014 (780853); turn right here for Benfleet station.**

31

West Horndon, Orsett and Bulphan

(Essex)

INFORMATION

Map OS 1:50,000 Landranger Sheet 177 'East London'.
Travel
  TRAIN (BR) – West Horndon.
  CAR – M25 to Jct 29; A127 towards Southend; A128 towards
    Orsett; in ½ mile, minor road on right to West Horndon.
    Park at station.
  Bus – Green Line (Victoria) 081 668–7261. Local
    Information: 0245 492211 (ext. 51587/51594). London
    Victoria–Grays–Orsett Hospital.
Length of walk 10 miles – circular – start and finish at West
  Horndon station (✂ *short cut* – 5½ miles).
Conditions Field paths and lanes. Careful navigation and
  attention to route instructions essential to locate plank
  bridges over dykes. Depending on season, ploughland or
  crops may obscure line of path and provide tiring walking.
  This ramble is for fit walkers, properly shod and with plenty
  of time – allow 5–6 hours.
Refreshments Railway Inn, West Horndon; Harrow Inn, near
  Bulphan; Foxhound or Whitmore Arms, Orsett.

This is a forgotten corner of south Essex, a wide swathe of flat farmland where the fields are bounded by ditches as well as hedges. The
whole area is reclaimed fenland, where under enormous skies the big
old farmhouses crouch behind their sheltering trees out in the middle
of nowhere, secretive and alluring. Few ramblers walk these lonely
paths – you're guaranteed a day away from it all in this unfrequented
landscape.

**From the platform at West Horndon station where you leave the
train from London (623881), cross the line by the footbridge and
go through the wicket gate beside the station sign. Follow the path**

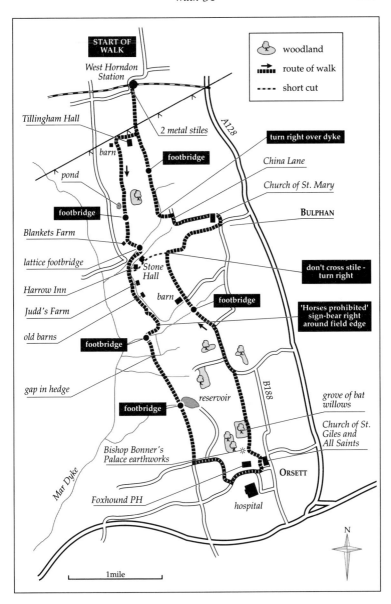

START OF WALK

West Horndon Station

Tillingham Hall

2 metal stiles

barn

footbridge

pond

A128

turn right over dyke

China Lane

Church of St. Mary

BULPHAN

footbridge

Blankets Farm

lattice footbridge

Stone Hall

don't cross stile - turn right

Harrow Inn

Judd's Farm

barn

footbridge

'Horses prohibited' sign-bear right around field edge

old barns

footbridge

gap in hedge

footbridge

reservoir

B188

grove of bat willows

Church of St. Giles and All Saints

Bishop Bonner's Palace earthworks

ORSETT

Mar Dyke

Foxhound PH

hospital

N

woodland

route of walk

short cut

1 mile

to the right, turn left along the road and immediately left again over two metal stiles. Pass a line of five trees in the field ahead to reach a farm road (623872); turn right to pass the farm buildings of Tillingham Hall and in 150 yards left beside a barn (621872 – yellow arrows) to walk due south.

This is quiet and windy country, where the farms lie like grounded ships among the wide, flat fields of potatoes and kale – rich farmland, reclaimed from fen and drained by deep dykes with rough plank footbridges across them. Pigeons clatter out of the tremendous oaks in the hedges, but there are few other sounds to spoil the solitude.

In the third field from the barn, leave a tree-lined pond on your right to find the plank bridge beyond; then aim to the left of Blankets Farm and cross a footbridge on to a lane (622856). Aim for a lattice footbridge and green footpath sign beyond, and turn right along the road (624854) past Stone Hall to turn left and reach the Harrow Inn (623852) with its vociferous three-legged dog and plush interior (✄ *short cut* – footpath behind the Harrow Inn leads past the back of Stone Hall to rejoin the walk ¾ mile from St Mary's Church at Bulphan). Continue along the rough lane ('PF 136' sign), past Judds Farm to some dilapidated barns.

The barns stand by a tributary channel of the Mar Dyke, which drains Bulphan and Orsett Fens. In the 19th century they stored farm produce which was loaded onto barges for London – the barges having come up the Mar Dyke from the Thames laden with horse manure from the London streets to spread on the south Essex farmlands.

A 'Public Footpath to Orsett' sign points ahead along a grassy path that reaches a 'Horses Prohibited' sign. Bear right here round a field edge to cross a plank footbridge 100 yards from the far right-hand corner of the field (625841). Cross the next field, aiming for a gap in the hedge; then another field, aiming for the big hospital building ahead, and keep the same line over the next field, steering for the right-hand corner of a reservoir's low embankment (631830). Cross the dyke and keep a hedge on your left as you walk south to a road (632820), where you turn left, and left again at the B188 (639818) into Orsett.

Nice old weatherboarded houses line Orsett's High Road, which leads past the hospital to the Church of St Giles and All Saints (church key – see notice in porch). St Giles's has a stumpy brick tower and a superb, tall Norman south doorway. It's a beautifully looked-after church, the pride of the village. The porch is of timber 600 years old; the nave is Norman; there is a simple stone bowl of a Saxon font. The rood screen was carved in 1911 out of timber from a frigate in which served one of the Bonham family of Orsett House. (In the churchyard stands a monument to the Bonhams, telling of two young men killed during the Great War, one at Jutland and the other at Gallipoli, and two more who died in the Second World War). At the west end of the south aisle are five 18th-century Italian plasterwork panels, showing exquisite craftsmanship and artistry combined, including a striking Resurrection

in which Christ leaps joyfully from his tomb, shroud flying, while two
Roman soldiers cower in mortal terror.

**'PF No. 110' points down a path beside the church tower; turn left
at the end, then right just before Pound Lane ('Bulphan' sign). The
ring-and-bailey earthworks of Bishop Bonner's Palace (641822) lie
behind trees on the left beyond the half-timbered Tudor wing of
Hall Farm. Walk through a grove of bat willows; then keep ahead
with a hedge on your right, to join a road (640835) and walk
ahead. At a sharp right-hand bend (636843) go straight on along
a field edge; where the accompanying hedge bends away left, walk
forward to another hedge and keep left of it to find the footbridge
100 yards left of the corner of the field. Go to the right of the barn
seen ahead on a farm lane (631848), cross a stile, and another in
the far left-hand corner of the following field. At the top of the
next field – a long one – don't cross the stile (✂ *short cut* – rejoins
here) but turn right (628854) to cross another stile and follow the
field edge to the left to reach the Church of St Mary at Bulphan
(637851).**

Bulphan (its name means 'burgh-fen: fortified settlement on the marshlands') has been settled since Saxon times. Its early Tudor church (key –
see notice in porch) is dominated by a thick-set tower under a pointed
little spire; the tower was hung with red tiles and furnished with a big,
bold clock to celebrate the Golden Jubilee of Queen Victoria. The base
of the tower is timbered, and the Tudor black oak porch is handsomely
carved. Inside is a 14th-century screen delicately fashioned in tracery.

**Turn left along the road for ⅓ mile (take care – this can be a busy
stretch), then right down China Lane (630859) past Slough House
Cottages – the end one is nicely pargetted with a wheat sheaf and
curious swallow-shaped motifs. In 15 yards turn left through a
hedge to cross a field and turn right over a dyke (627860). Where
the dyke bends right keep ahead, and just before the top of the field
cross a ditch on your right, continuing to walk north to reach the
farm road at Tillingham Hall (624872). A footpath sign points
ahead to the five trees and the metal stiles that lead back to West
Horndon station.**

32

Sutton-at-Hone, Horton Kirby and the River Darent
(Kent)

INFORMATION

Map OS 1:50,000 Landranger Sheet 177 'East London'.
Travel
> TRAIN (BR) – Farningham Road.
> CAR – M25 to Jct 3; A20 towards Maidstone for 1 mile; A225 north towards Dartford for 1½ miles to Farningham Road station on left. Park near station.

Length of walk 5 miles – roughly figure-of-eight – start and finish at Farningham Road station.
Conditions Riverside and field paths, lanes and elevated causeway.
Opening times St John's Jerusalem, Sutton-at-Hone closed at time of writing due to what the National Trust terms 'unforeseen circumstances'. Usually open in summer, April–end October. For details, ring 0892 890651.
Refreshments Sun Inn, South Darenth; Fighting Cocks, Horton Kirby.
Reading Booklet available (in normal circumstances!) at St John's Jerusalem.

Only three miles south of Dartford and the industrial Thames, the River Darent might be in deepest rural Kent as it twists its way down a green valley overlooked by hills, woods and farms. There are flooded gravel pits full of wildfowl, splendid old paper mills and an ancient house, once the headquarters of an order of crusader knights and now in the care of the National Trust.

At Farningham Road station (556693) cross the line by the foot-bridge, walk down the station approach road and cross the A225 into a road which leads in ¼ mile to a bridge over the River Darent (563693).

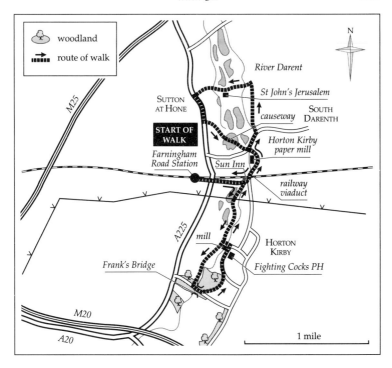

An impressive railway viaduct spans the valley here, overshadowing Horton Kirby paper mill just downstream – now housing small businesses. Below the viaduct crouches the Sun Inn, a good place to return to after the walk.

Upstream the river is flanked by big gravel pits, now flooded to form lakes where ducks, geese and moorhens clamour.

Turn right off the road just before the bridge (yellow arrow waymark) along the west bank of the Darent, and follow the river for ½ mile to a disused mill (560684). Here the path leaves the river to follow a field edge, rejoining it at the corner of a wood (557682). Follow the river to the road by the squat, brick Frank's Bridge (556679), where you turn left and in 50 yards left again (stile and footpath sign). Follow the edge of the wood to a road (560680), and bear left to walk through Horton Kirby village.

Like its sister villages of Sutton-at-Hone and South Darenth, Horton Kirby's main employment was until recently in the paper mills on the Darent. These days most of the inhabitants of its attractive brick and flint houses commute to work much further afield, but it still retains a rural village atmosphere. The local foxhounds meet from time to time at the Fighting Cocks pub.

Bear left beyond the Fighting Cocks to cross the river by the old mill, and turn right to return to the Sun Inn. Take the road to the right of the pub, under the arch of the viaduct, past the paper mill and the Jolly Miller pub. On a right-hand bend bear left (563699) on a fenced path that leads to the river bank.

In ½ mile a footbridge over the river (562704) leads to a muddy track which meets the A255 in Sutton-at-Hone (555703). Turn left here for ¼ mile to reach the gates of St John's Jerusalem on the left (557702).

The house of St John's Jerusalem (559704) is a remarkable place, full of history. The oldest part of the building is the chapel of 1234, now incorporated in the east end of the house, but the Knights Hospitallers of the Order of St John of Jerusalem were settled here a good century before the chapel was built, in a local 'commandery' or headquarters. The Order was established after Jerusalem had been captured for the first time by the Crusaders, to care for the sick and to keep in military trim for the crushing of Islam. The Knights Hospitallers saw their Order dissolved in 1540, along with all the other monastic orders of England, and their house passed through many private hands until Abraham Hill – who lived here for the best part of 60 years, between 1665 and 1721 – extended and altered it to the comfortable gentleman's residence it now appears. The grounds it stands in are superbly kept, with great cedars of Lebanon, copper beeches and flowering cherry trees.

From St John's gate walk left down the A225 for 200 yards to turn left beside No. 117, Clare Cottage (558700 – footpath sign) on to a causeway between the flooded pits which leads back to the Sun Inn and Farningham Road station.

33

Great Expectations Country – Higham, Cooling and the Marshes (Kent)

INFORMATION

Map OS 1:50,000 Landranger Sheet 178 'The Thames Estuary'.

Travel

>TRAIN (BR) – Higham.

>CAR – M25 to Jct 2; A2; A289 (¾ mile beyond A2/M2 jct); A226 towards Gravesend; turn right in 1 mile through Higham to Higham station. Park at station.

Length of walk 17 miles – circular – start and finish at Higham station.

Conditions Lanes, sea wall and field paths. Sea wall path narrow and slippery in places; some field paths between Cooling and Lower Higham may be under plough. Walking boots recommended. Take binoculars for river and marsh birds and views. This walk is for fit walkers with plenty of stamina.

Opening times Sun Inn, Church Street – weekday evenings 7–11; weekends lunchtime as well.

Refreshments Chequers, Lower Higham; Sun Inn, Church Street; Horseshoe and Castle, Cooling.

Reading

>*Great Expectations* by Charles Dickens.

>*Discover Dickens's Kent* – from Dickens House, 48 Doughty Street, London WC1N 2LF.

Lonely churches and villages on the southern shore of the Thames estuary punctuate this long walk, which offers you wide views over marsh and river and a real sense of solitude, as well as the chance of some good bird-watching. The core of the walk is Charles Dickens's *Great Expectations*, for this is where he set the most dramatic scenes of his masterpiece.

From Higham station (715726) turn right over the railway and pass the Chequers pub to walk the lonely mile north to the hamlet of Church Street and St Mary's Church (716742).

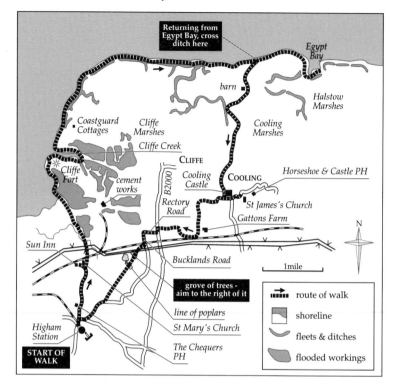

Charles Dickens used many local places as background for *Great Expectations*, and it was in the churchyard of St Mary's that the convict Magwitch turned Pip upside down so that the steeple flew under his feet. The desolation of the marshland scene hereabouts that lent such a sinister air to Dickens's description has diminished since 1860, thanks to the advent of electricity pylons and railway. But St Mary's with its walls striped in alternate bands of flint and stone, and its wonderfully carved 600-year-old south door, is still a lonely church (and nowadays an unused one) in a very lonely spot.

The Sun Inn (no name-board), run by Mr Vidler, is just along the lane south of the church – a perfect, unspoilt country pub.

Pass the fine old barn opposite the church, cross the railway (717744), bear right through a gate and follow yellow arrow way-marks to the left of the big cement works, between a creek and a flooded pit. Turn left along a bank (712755) on a deteriorating path to reach Cliffe Fort (706762).

The fort was erected in 1870 on the site of the old battery that Dickens knew, which had been built in 1539 by King Henry VIII against the threat of French invasion. Here Pip ran through the fog on Christmas morning to bring 'wittles' and a file to Magwitch; here he spent Sunday afternoons with his brother-in-law, the mild-mannered and much put-upon Joe Gargery; here he upset poor Biddy with his grand talk. Near here stood the gibbet for pirate corpses that so horrified young Pip.

The fort, a grim ruin with blank windows and overgrown courtyard, looks out over the wide Thames to the flaring chimneys of the oil refineries of Shell Haven on the Essex shore.

Pass to the right of the fort and bend right around Cliffe Creek. At the head of the creek bear left (715769) to follow the sea wall past gloomy old coastguard cottages and on around the edge of Cliffe and Cooling Marshes for five blissfully lonely miles, looking north over the widening Thames and south across the flat, wind-swept marshland, to reach Egypt Bay (775790).

In this isolated bay of mud and marsh where shelduck and curlew feed undisturbed, Dickens saw the coastguard ship *Swallow* moored, and sited his own creation in the same spot, the terrible Hulks to which the runaway convicts Magwitch and Compeyson were returned after being captured while fighting each other. From here the cannon boomed across the marshes to let the villagers know of escaped prisoners.

Retrace your steps for a mile to the first crossing over the ditch inside the sea wall (760792) and follow a gravelly track for 2½ miles, past a barn and across the marshes to a road (752759), where you turn left to find Cooling Castle and St James's Church. The Horseshoe and Castle pub is a little further along the road.

The gatehouse towers of Cooling Castle (753759) face the road. The castle was built in 1380 to defend the port of Cliffe against French raids. Its moated grounds are haunted by the ghost of Sir John Oldcastle, burned as a heretic in 1417 and said to be the model for Shakespeare's Falstaff.

St James's Church (756760) contains some very ancient pews – perhaps 600 years old. Beside the porch are 13 little stone lozenge-shaped tombs of infants of the Baker and Comport families who died of marsh ague between 1771 and 1800. Dickens's imagination transported these tombs to St Mary's at Church Street as the brothers of Pip, whose childish belief (from their shape) was that 'they had all been born on their backs with their hands in their trousers-pockets'.

Returning to Cooling Castle, the road bends to reach a junction (745758); turn left to pass Gattons Farm and turn right beside the railway (745749). In 300 yards bear right, then left across fields to the B2000 (735751). Turn left and immediately right down Rectory Road, then left along Bucklands Road (731750) for 250 yards to cross the railway and turn right over a stile (731746 –

yellow arrow). Cross a field diagonally, aiming to the right of a grove of trees; cross two footbridges and go diagonally across a field to pass through a line of poplars and cross a stile, then another ahead over a farm road (726740). Keep ahead over fields and another track, sticking to the same line until you meet a road (721732), where you turn right to reach the Chequers pub and Higham station.

34

Isle of Sheppey – Harty Marshes, Shell Ness and the Swale Nature Reserve
(Kent)

INFORMATION

Map OS 1:50,000 Landranger Sheet 178 'The Thames Estuary'.
Travel CAR – M25 to Jct 2; A2 to M2; M2 to Jct 5; A249
   towards Sheerness; on Isle of Sheppey, at first roundabout
   turn right on B2231 for 3½ miles to roundabout at
   Eastchurch; continue on B2231 for 1½ miles to turn right on
   minor road. In 2½ miles bend sharp right at Elliotts Farm,
   then sharp left at drive to Mocketts Farm to reach St
   Thomas's Church. Park at church.
Length of walk 6 miles – circular – start and finish at St
   Thomas's Church.
Conditions Farm tracks and sea wall path, often wet and
   muddy. Bring binoculars and bird book.
Refreshments Ferry House Inn.
Reading Notes available in St Thomas's Church.

This is a walk in a landscape remote and windswept enough to rival the Dengie peninsula ramble (No. 29). The Isle of Sheppey is one of those places tourists don't visit, and the Harty Marshes on their south-eastern tip are some of the loneliest acres in the south of England. Where humans don't go, however, the birds do, and this is incomparable bird-watching territory. St Thomas's is Kent's most isolated church; the Ferry Inn its remotest pub. You can't get further away from it all than here in this wild and magical spot.

Sheppey was a forgotten island until the Kingsferry Bridge opened in 1860, a place of smugglers and inward-looking inhabitants, seldom visited by the outside world except for the naval dockyard at Sheerness. Down in the flat marshlands of the south-east corner of Sheppey you can still feel as lonely as anywhere in England. A handful of widely separated farmhouses is scattered amid vast acres of sheep and cattle grazing, whipped by the sea wind which flattens and tilts the sheltering trees.

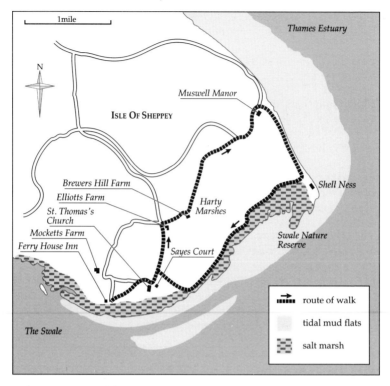

1 mile

Thames Estuary

N

Muswell Manor

ISLE OF SHEPPEY

Shell Ness

Brewers Hill Farm
Elliotts Farm   *Harty*
St. Thomas's   *Marshes*
Church
Mocketts Farm   *Swale Nature*
Ferry House Inn   *Reserve*
                    Sayes Court

route of walk

tidal mud flats

salt marsh

The Swale

The little Norman church of St Thomas looks over the grey waters of the choppy Swale channel that separates Sheppey from the Kentish shore. There's a tiny bell-cote on the roof and a dark interior hung with oil lights. The Lady Chapel on the south side, however, is flooded by daylight through a large window. In this chapel stands a beautiful oak chest made early in the 15th century by a Flemish or German craftsman, carved with figures of jousting knights. No one knows how it came to rest in St Thomas's, but local legend says it was found floating in the Swale.

From St Thomas's Church (022662) and Sayes Court Farm next door, follow the lane northwards to pass Elliotts Farm and turn right (025674) along a track past Brewers Hill Farm (030675) and on across Harty Marshes.

Recent changes in the agriculture of Sheppey have seen some of these old grazing marshes ploughed up for arable farming: profitable for the farmers, but disastrous for the huge numbers of shelduck and other ducks and geese that roost and feed on the grasslands in winter. Hen harriers, kestrels and short-eared owls hunt the marshes, but their victims – the mice and small birds attracted by the marsh plants and insects – are disappearing as their food source goes under the plough. Who will win this battle for territory – man or nature?

Continue from Brewers Hill Farm for 1½ miles to reach Muswell Manor (043695).

This house, now the centre of a mobile home park, was the headquarters of the Royal Flying Club back in 1910 – Lord Brabazon, Winston Churchill and the Hon C.S. Rolls all came here to pilot their stringbag biplanes above the marshes.

Bear right at the manor to reach the sea wall (047693), turning right along the grassy path for a mile to reach the hamlet of Shell Ness (052682).

The views from the sea wall are superb, spreading over many shining miles of Thames estuary to the coastal towns on the low Kent coastline. On the spit of land at Shell Ness a row of old coastguard cottages looks out over a carpet of shells and pebbles; next to them runs a short street of holiday houses, lovingly maintained by owners who enjoy windy weekends of walking, painting and bird-watching.

Salt marshes and mud flats stretch away on your left, the winter food larder of up to 20,000 waders – dunlin, knot, bar-tailed godwits, oystercatchers, curlew, plovers. They swirl over the enormous skies in great clouds, twisting and turning all together. Dark-bellied brent geese winter here, too, feeding on eel-grass. Redshank, gadwall and pochard breed in the reserve. This is a wonderful place to walk and observe.

From Shell Ness continue along the sea wall path through the Swale Nature Reserve. After 2½ miles the path turns inland (032662) to reach Sayes Court and St Thomas's Church. Just beyond the building a track on the left leads down to the Ferry House Inn (015660).

Parts of the inn date back 500 years. For centuries the Ferry House Inn catered for travellers reaching the Isle of Sheppey by ferry across the Swale. Nowadays it's an excellent pub for food and beer, with a memorable view across the water as sauce for your meal.

35

Newington
and Lower Halstow
(Kent)

INFORMATION

Map OS 1:50,000 Landranger Sheet 178 'The Thames Estuary'.
Travel
  TRAIN (BR) – Newington.
  CAR – M25 to Jct 2; A2; M2 to Jct 5; A249 towards
      Sittingbourne; A2 towards London for 1½ miles. Park at
      Newington station.
Length of walk 6½ miles – circular – start and finish at
  Newington station.
Conditions Lanes, sea wall, field and orchard paths. Bring
  binoculars for Medway estuary views.
Opening times
  St Mary's Church, Newington Easter– October, weekends 2–4.
      At other times, key from vicarage in Church Lane (150
      yards beyond railway bridge, on left).
  St Margaret's Church, Lower Halstow 9.30 each morning for
      a short while. At other times, key from Mill House next to
      Three Tuns pub, or telephone vicar (0634 387227).
Refreshments Bull, George or Wheatsheaf Inns, Newington;
  Three Tuns, Lower Halstow; Crown, Upchurch.

Three notable old churches stand along the course of this walk, which runs through the apple and plum orchards and along the sea wall of one of the marshy-edged peninsulas that protrude into the estuary of the River Medway. North of Lower Halstow there are wide views over the estuary, best at low tide when miles of green weed, mud and sand flats are exposed, gleaming with creeks and pools of water.

From Newington station (859650) turn left along an alleyway opposite No. 41 Station Road, left into Church Lane and right in ¼ mile at a crossroads (860653 – 'Iwade' sign) to pass Church Farm House with its oasts and half-timbered rear portion and reach the church of St Mary the Virgin (862653).

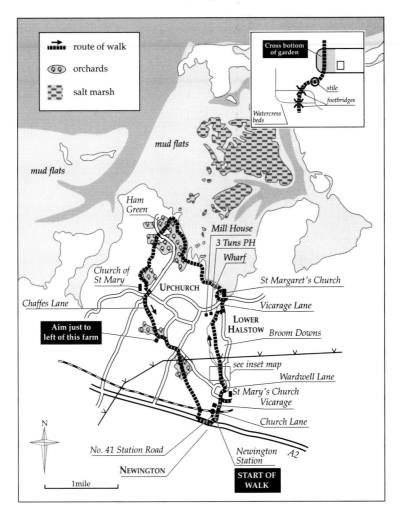

route of walk

orchards

salt marsh

Cross bottom of garden

stile

footbridges

Watercress beds

mud flats

mud flats

Ham Green

Mill House

3 Tuns PH

Wharf

Church of St Mary

UPCHURCH

St Margaret's Church

Chaffes Lane

Vicarage Lane

Aim just to left of this farm

LOWER HALSTOW

Broom Downs

see inset map

Wardwell Lane

St Mary's Church

Vicarage

Church Lane

N

No. 41 Station Road

Newington Station

A2

NEWINGTON

START OF WALK

1 mile

The weather-beaten tower of St Mary's, striped in bands of flint and ragstone, dominates the nearby countryside. This is a remarkable church, well worth the effort of seeking out the key (see information box p. 130). Among many treasures it contains a lovely spidery purlin roof 700 years old over the south chancel, a brass in the chancel floor showing Lady Cobham in full Elizabethan dress, a huge, iron-banded trunk chest and some humorously carved devils on a 15th-century priest's desk. But the church's chief glory is its wonderful display of wall paintings of about 1340 AD on the north and north-east walls. These include an epic Judgement Day with the righteous rising from sheltered coffins at the blast of trumpets blown by two angels, while the damned bare their teeth in the agonies inflicted by a horrifically masked devil.

There is also a Nativity with a shawled Virgin and a figure of St Joseph stroking his brow, overcome with awe; and saints painted on the window splays, one of them a bald and luxuriantly bearded St Paul with a sensual mouth and large, expressive eyes.

Don't miss this treat of a church.

At the church gate lies a sarsen stone known as the Devil's Stone. Local legend says that the devil, disturbed by the church bells, jumped from the tower with the bells in his sack, landed on the stone and rolled down the hill into a stream.

Return to the crossroads, turn right into Wardwell Lane and in 250 yards left (861654 – concrete footpath sign) to cross two foot-bridges over watercress beds (now dry) and turn right over a stile. Bear left along the bottom of a garden and continue over stiles to climb a hill to a pylon (860661); then walk forward over the back of Broom Downs, aiming dead ahead to the left of ramshackle sheds at the far end of an enormous field where a stile leads into a road at Lower Halstow (859669). Turn left and immediately right along a stream-side path to go right in 300 yards up Westmorland Drive, right at a junction along Crouch Hill Court, left up Vicarage Lane, right at the T-junction and in 100 yards left past Church House to St Margaret's Church (860675).

The walls of St Margaret's are a crazy mixture of Roman tiles (there were Roman tile and brick works at Lower Halstow), stones and flints. The stumpy tower has a pointed cap, and the tiled roof slopes on the north side almost to ground level. Unfortunately the church is kept locked, but after fetching the key from Mill House next to the Three Tuns pub you can admire the nave (late Saxon or early Norman) and remnants of medieval wall paintings.

Saxon monks named Lower Halstow 'Halig Stow', the holy place. There was a busy brickworks on the wharf beyond the church until recently, but these days you walk past a grassy area on to the sea wall, where the Saxon Shore Way footpath runs north along the peninsula, with views over the Medway estuary, a huge expanse of mud flats whose islets stand clear of the mud, covered in mats of brown seaweed and green spikes of glasswort. Barges converted to snug dwellings lie up in the creeks, while inland the apple orchards stretch away to lonely farmhouses.

A mile north of Lower Halstow the path turns inland at an inlet (850691 – yellow arrow waymark) to Ham Green. Bear right at the road (847688) and immediately left through an orchard; keep ahead to a stile at the bottom and along a fenced path to a lane (845681). Turn left, and in 300 yards right over a stile through an orchard. Go over two stiles to bear left around another orchard, over another stile to turn left up steps, left through a housing estate

and right at the road to reach the Church of St Mary at Upchurch (844675).

St Mary's spire features one 'candle-snuffer' on top of another. Inside, the south wall has a 14th-century chalk arcade with lions and a green man with flowers in his mouth, some lovely medieval glass showing an angel playing what looks like a hurdy-gurdy (south chancel) and superb blue glass (north aisle), a list of vicars including Edmund Drake (1560–67), father of Sir Francis Drake, and on the south wall a 13th-century painting of St Spiridon of Cyprus pouring gold pieces from his chasuble – he had turned a snake into gold to help a poor farmer, and reconverted the gold into a snake when the farmer returned the money to him.

From the church continue along the main street, turning left opposite the post office down Chaffes Lane and in 200 yards left opposite Bradshaws Close (844672), across a field. In 200 yards bear left through a hedge and keep the same line over a stile and across fields to cross a stile and walk round the edge of an orchard to a stile, from which you aim just to the left of a farm below to reach a road (849665). Turn right to the crossroads (851663), cross and go over a stile, aiming for a pylon and then straight up the hill over more stiles, through orchards on the same line to another stile. Go diagonally right over a field to a stile and on to cross a road (853655), continuing across fields towards Newington's railway platforms ahead. Go under the railway arch (856650) and on between Nos. 11 and 13 to turn left along the A2 back to the station.

36

Cobham
and Luddesdown
(Kent)

INFORMATION

Map OS 1:50,000 Landranger Sheet 177 'East London'.
Travel
    TRAIN (BR) – Nearest station Sole Street (1½ miles).
    CAR – M25 to Jct 2; A2 towards Rochester; 1 mile beyond
        Gravesend turn-off (A227) minor road signed 'Cobham';
        park at Leather Bottle Inn.
    BUS – Green Line (Victoria) 081 668–7261. Local
        information: 0800 (Freephone) 696996.
        London Victoria–Gravesend–Cobham; bus stops at war
        memorial along village street from church, or outside
        Leather Bottle on request.
Length of walk 6 miles – circular – start and finish at the
    Leather Bottle Inn, Cobham.
Conditions Field paths, lanes and woodland tracks. Path to
    mausoleum in Cobham Park can be very muddy.
Refreshments Leather Bottle Inn or Darnley Arms, Cobham;
    Golden Lion, Luddesdown.
Reading
    Pickwick Papers by Charles Dickens (Everyman).
    The River and the Downs by Michael Baldwin (Gollancz).
    Cobham booklets, available in Cobham church.

The village of Cobham is full of interest – plenty of associations with Charles Dickens, a church containing the finest collection of memorial brasses in the world, and the 14th-century Cobham College, now a characterful home for elderly people. Luddesdown, two miles to the south, enjoys an idyllic setting in the Kent countryside and has the oldest continuously inhabited house in Britain; while Cobham Park holds the eerie, never-completed mausoleum of the Darnley family hidden among its fine old trees.

The Leather Bottle Inn in Cobham was the setting chosen by Charles

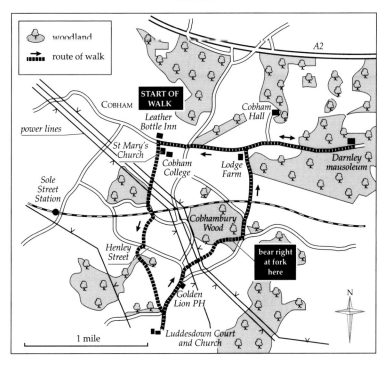

Dickens for Mr Pickwick's mercy dash to the lovelorn Tracey Tupman, supposedly suicidal after being jilted by Rachael Wardle. Mr Pickwick spent a wakeful night at the inn, and just down the street made his historic discovery of the ancient stone inscribed 'Bil Stumps His Mark'. The stone – or another just like it! – still stands outside the inn, which is filled with Dickens memorabilia that include several examples of the great man's signature.

Opposite the inn, St Mary's Church contains a unique collection of memorial brasses to the de Cobham lords of the manor and their ladies, from the early 14th to the early 16th centuries. The brasses form a softly glowing pavement in the chancel, among them the matronly figure of Dame Jone de Kobeham (1298), Sir John de Cobham in full armour, holding a model of the church he rebuilt in 1367, and slim-waisted Lady Joan (1433) in long-sleeved widow's weeds. Above them lie the splendid alabaster Elizabethan effigies of George Brooke, Lord Cobham, his wife Anne and their ten sons and four daughters.

Behind the church stands a square of old stone houses round a peaceful, grassy quadrangle. They were originally built in 1362 by Sir John de Cobham as a college for priests to say mass for his ancestors. In 1598 they became almshouses, and still shelter elderly men and women today.

From the Leather Bottle (670685), pass to the right of the church and Cobham College, and take a track down the left hand side of the new graveyard to a stile and a path that crosses a field under power lines to a road (668676). Turn left to cross the railway and immediately bear right in front of a house, following a hedge and field path down to the road at Henley Street (666672). Opposite and slightly to the left you cross a stile (yellow arrow waymark), climb up through woodland (667670) and descend to the road at Luddesdown (670662). Walk ahead to find the church and Luddesdown Court.

Seen from the hillside, Luddesdown looks the perfect picture of Kentish contentment – venerable church and Luddesdown Court huddled together among trees in their steep-sided valley. The Court was built just after the Norman Conquest by Odo, Bishop of Bayeux, and still contains its great hall, solar and ladies' bower at the core of a jumble of many centuries' architecture. It's said to be the oldest house in Britain in continuous occupation.

Return to the grass triangle where three roads meet and bear right to the Golden Lion pub (672666); turn left here (Cobham sign), right in 200 yards through a hedge (yellow arrow) and cross a field under power lines to turn right inside the edge of Cobhambury Wood (676672). In 150 yards the path forks; electricity poles continue ahead up a ride, but bear right under trees to a road (680672). Turn left here (Cobham sign), right in 200 yards, under the railway (681677) and reach a track at Lodge Farm (681683), where you turn right.

Cobham Hall, below you in the valley (683689), is part Elizabethan and part Stuart, a huge and handsome house which the Brooke family lost when it backed Sir Walter Raleigh in his 1603 plot to dethrone King James I. (The plot cost Sir Walter and Sir George Brooke their heads.) The park, laid out by the celebrated landscape designer Sir Humphry Repton in the 1790s, is full of splendid old oaks, sweet chestnuts and limes. Charles Dickens often came across from his home at Gad's Hill to walk here.

A mile along the track stands the mausoleum (695683) designed in 1783 by James Wyatt for the Darnley family who succeeded the Brookes at Cobham Hall. Crowned with a pyramid and surrounded by classical columns, the derelict mausoleum contains shelves in its cold, dark heart that were intended for generations of Darnley coffins. But the mausoleum was never used – the Bishop of Rochester refused to consecrate it, disturbed by the bad omen of a thunderstorm when the foundation stone was being laid.

From the mausoleum walk back along the path through the woods to Cobham.

37

Coldrum Stones, Pilgrims' Way and Harvel
(Kent)

INFORMATION

Map OS 1:50,000 Landranger Sheet 177 'East London'.

Travel CAR – M25 to Jct 3; M20; A227 towards Gravesend; turn right at Vigo Inn (2 miles) to Trottiscliffe; left in village to pass church and bear left to Coldrum Long Barrow car park.

Length of walk 5 miles – circular – start and finish at Coldrum Long Barrow car park.

Conditions Rough, muddy woodland paths and byways. Take tree and flower books.

Refreshments Vigo Inn; Amazon and Tiger, Harvel.

Reading
  A Guide to the Pilgrim's Way and North Downs Way by Christopher John Wright (Constable).
  The Old Road by Hilaire Belloc (1904).

These paths and trackways, commanding superb views from Trosley Down over the Weald of Kent, run through ancient woodland and up into rolling farmland. Part of the route lies along the prehistoric pathway of the Pilgrims' Way, a delightful stroll through shady tunnels of trees. You visit a neolithic long barrow and the out-of-the-way village of Harvel along the route, as well as one of Kent's few genuinely unspoiled and hospitable pubs.

From the Coldrum Long Barrow car park (650607) follow the signs to Coldrum Long Barrow (654607).

This neolithic long barrow was built in about 2,000 BC. The remains of 22 people of that date have been unearthed here. Half of the original circle of upright stones, 60 feet in circumference, has fallen away, leaving four big sarsens standing on the edge of the knoll surrounded by a semi-circle of fallen stones, of purple-grey sandstone not found locally. Ash, beech and field maple enclose the knoll, adding to its seclusion.

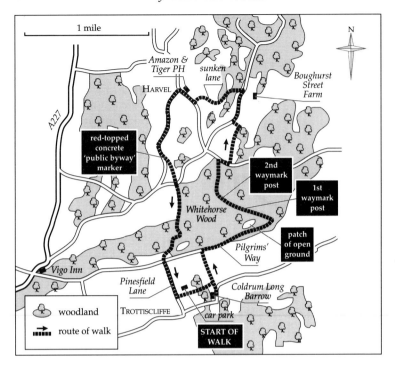

Descend the steps and turn left to climb up to the Pilgrims' Way (652612) along which you turn to the right.

The modern North Downs Way footpath coincides for much of its length with the Pilgrims' Way. Pilgrims journeying to the tomb of St Thomas à Becket at Canterbury certainly used the Way from medieval times onwards; but this is a high-level route, connecting the ancient settlements on the Wiltshire plains with the continent, which has been trodden since prehistoric times. 'The Old Road', Hilaire Belloc called it in his account of his journey along the Pilgrims' Way at the turn of the century, and walking here, looking out over the Weald of Kent between the yews and field maples, you get a real sense of the weight of history attached to it.

In ½ mile the Pilgrims' Way passes an open piece of ground on the left, white with exposed chalk. Two hundred yards beyond, you reach a post with yellow arrows, one pointing forward, another to the left (662616). Turn left here, steeply up steps, to climb Trosley Down through the jungly Whitehorse Wood.

There are stunning views across 20 miles of Kent between the trees of this unmanaged tangle of old chalk down woodland. Ash, beech, field maple, elder, hazel, thorn trees, spindle, wild service trees, limes, way-faring tree and enormous old yews – these are only a sample of what's growing here. The top of the down is covered in sweet chestnut coppice.

Pass a waymark post, and in ¼ mile turn right at the next (655620) to turn right at a road (655624). In 50 yards go left over a stile (public footpath sign) and follow a fence on your left, over a stile to turn left at another stile (yellow 'WW' arrow) and walk with a hedge on your right to a road (657629). Turn right, and in ¼ mile left up a bridleway opposite Boughurst Street Farm (659633). Walk ahead and along the edge of woodland to climb a sunken lane and turn left along a farm track to a road (652631). Turn right into Harvel.

Thatched roofs, pointed oasts, brick and flint cottages peeping from trees, a duckpond and the Amazon and Tiger pub – these make up Harvel, a neat little village rather off the beaten track. But Harvel has had its moments – Michael Baldwin in his wonderfully cranky book *The River and the Downs* (Gollancz 1984) tells of the Harvel poultry-keeper brought to justice in the not-too-distant past for raping and strangling his pullets. It helped to pass the time in those long pre-television evenings.

Turn left opposite the Amazon and Tiger pub, ignoring tempting footpaths each side, to take a public byway on the left in ⅔ mile (648625 – red-topped concrete marker). Cross a T-junction (650621) and walk forward for ½ mile. Another red-topped marker points off to the right, but keep forward along a muddy lane to turn right in 200 yards between wooden posts (650613). Drop downhill through trees for 300 yards to take a path on the left, steeply descending the face of the down to reach the Pilgrims' Way (649611) and walk forward down Pinesfield Lane, turning left (650607) to reach the Coldrum Long Barrow car park.

The Vigo Inn (631610) is the perfect place to refuel after the walk. There's no piped music, fruit machine or pretentious menu – just simple food, well-kept beer and good conversation in an old-fashioned bar. Long may it continue thus.

·38·

Shoreham
and Otford
(Kent)

INFORMATION

Map OS 1:50,000 Landranger Sheet 188 'Maidstone and the
Weald of Kent'.
Travel
    TRAIN (BR) – Shoreham
    CAR – M25 to Jct 4; A224 towards Sevenoaks; at Badger's
    Mount (1 mile) turn left on minor road to Shoreham.
    Park at Shoreham station.
Length of walk 6 miles – circular – start and finish at Shoreham
    station.
Conditions Roads, woodland and field paths.
Opening times Shoreham Countryside Centre, Shoreham station
    April–October, Saturdays and Bank Holidays 2.30–5.30;
    Sundays 11–5.
Refreshments George Inn, Shoreham; Crown, Otford.

There are no lovelier sections of the Darent Valley than these few miles
between the downs. Shoreham village has been adored by several
generations of painters, while further down the valley in the village of
Otford stands the remnant of a magnificent residence of a Tudor
Archbishop of Canterbury.

**Turn right down the steps from the station (525615) and right
again under the bridge to reach Shoreham village and its Church
of St Peter and St Paul (522616).**

The church porch entrance, reached down a yew avenue, was hewn
from a single oak tree root. In a painting hanging on the west wall
inside the church, a Victorian vicar of Shoreham waits outside the
porch to welcome Lieutenant Verney Lovett Cameron, R.N., arriving
home in a tremendous triumphal car (apparently drawn by most of the
village) after making the first east-west crossing of Africa in 1873–5.

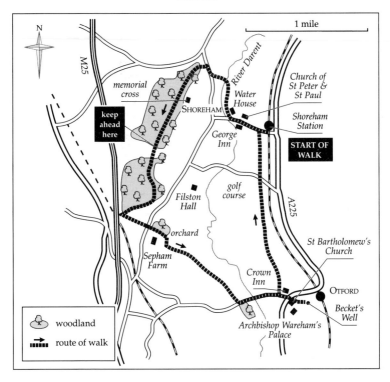

Art is well represented in the church, from the superb fan-vaulted 15th-century dark wood rood screen to the 1903 window by Sir Edward Burne-Jones in memory of geologist Sir Joseph Prestwich, which features Creation as an angel holding a globe swirling with sun, moon and sea. There's also a delicate head of Christ by Harold Copping, one of the large number of artists drawn to Shoreham over the past two centuries. William Blake (1757–1827), the visionary painter and poet, stayed at Water House further down the village street, as did Samuel Palmer from 1827 to 1834 as one of a group of Blake's pupils known as The Ancients. Palmer's watercolours of landscapes, buildings and trees celebrated this peaceful part of rural Kent.

Walk down the street from the church to bear right along Darenth Way before the bridge over the River Darent. Water House stands here white and solid behind its hedge and wall (520616). By the bridge a memorial to Shoreham's dead in the First World War directs your gaze up to the hillside opposite, where a cross was cut out of the turf in commemoration (subsequent tree growth has obscured the view from the bridge). Follow the path beside the Darent to cross the river (520621) and bear left up a lane to a T-junction. Turn right here (take care – narrow road with sharp

bends), and in 250 yards left (518622 – yellow arrow waymark) up a track that meets a lane. Turn back sharply here to your left along a trackway that runs along the hillside, past a pole barrier and on south-west above the memorial cross in the turf (515618). There are wonderful views from this hillside over Shoreham and the Darent valley, laid out at your feet.

Where the trees end, yellow arrows point downhill (511612), but keep ahead on the same contour, looking down on the white-capped oasts and tall red chimneys of Filston Hall. The path descends to the lower edge of the wood (511603) and keeps along it towards the M25 motorway, hidden from view in a cutting. What would our ancestors have made of the roaring noise emanating from this seemingly deserted hillside? The path re-enters trees just before reaching the motorway (506603); turn left here down the slope to a stile and follow a line of electricity poles to the left of the oasts at Sepham Farm (510600). At the end of an orchard bear right, then left on a rough track; where this swings left keep ahead for ½ mile across fields to a road (521592), where you turn left to cross the Darent and walk up Otford's pretty High Street to a roundabout (528593).

Handsome houses overlook the village duckpond, marooned nowadays at the centre of the roundabout, backed by the stumpy tower of St Bartholomew's Church. Another tower stands nearby, octagonal in brick and stone, its mullioned windows staring blankly – all that remains of the once magnificent palace built by a Tudor Archbishop of Canterbury as a staging-post on his frequent journeys between Canterbury and London. Archbishop Wareham's palace at Otford was an enormous structure, 440 feet by 220 feet. King Henry VIII brought a retinue of 4,000 with him, and another 1,000 to look after his Queen Katherine, when he stayed here in May 1520 on his way to the historic 'Field of the Cloth of Gold' meeting in France. But the hospitality he enjoyed on that occasion did not prevent the palace's destruction 20 years later at the Reformation.

If you pass the south side of the church and the newer graveyard, you'll find on the right of the footpath the remains of Becket's Well. This well probably dates back to Roman times or earlier, but local legend says that it was struck out of the ground with a staff, Moses-style, by Archbishop Thomas à Becket, in a fury at the lack of water while building a manor house here.

Retrace your steps past the pond and the Crown Inn, and in 50 yards turn right ('Shoreham' footpath sign) along a farm road. Continue ahead where it turns left (525600), through fields and a golf course, across a lane (524608) and on between barbed wire fences to turn right at a road (524615) and return to Shoreham station.

·39·

Plaxtol, Ightham Mote
and Oldbury Fort
(Kent)

INFORMATION

Map OS 1:50,000 Landranger Sheet 188 'Maidstone and the Weald of Kent'.

Travel

TRAIN (BR) – Borough Green and Wrotham.

CAR – M25 to Jct 5; A21 to A25 (1 mile); A25 towards Maidstone; A227 at Borough Green to railway station. Park at station.

BUS – Green Line (Victoria) 081 668–7261. Local information: 0800 (Freephone) 696996. London Victoria–Gravesend–Borough Green and Wrotham BR station.

Length of walk 8½ miles – circular – start and finish at Borough Green and Wrotham station.

Conditions Lanes, field and woodland paths. Muddy and wet underfoot in Mill Lane below Basted, woods around Fairlawne and sunken track on Oldbury Hill. Ascent from road at 580546 up Raspit Hill is very steep. Reasonably fit walkers only; walking boots recommended.

Opening Times Ightham Mote House (NT) April–October (inclusive); closed Tuesdays and Saturdays.

Refreshments The Forge, Plaxtol; The Cob Tree, Ightham (on A25); The Tea House, Borough Green.

Reading Ightham Mote booklets available at the house.

These footpaths and bridleways lead through the oak, sweet chestnut and silver birch woodlands and the steep fields and orchards of the northern Kentish Weald, with the moated Tudor house of Ightham Mote as a focal point. But there are more treats along the way – the Cromwellian church with no name at Plaxtol, an enormous Iron Age fort on Oldbury Hill and ancient trackways sunk deep among the trees.

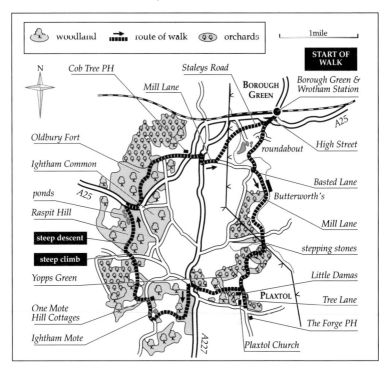

From **Borough Green and Wrotham station (609574)** turn right
over the bridge down Borough Green's High Street to cross the A25
and continue ahead past Basted sign to a roundabout. Follow
Basted and Plaxtol signs under a bridge (605568) along a hollow
lane, turning right at the top of a rise down Basted Lane (604563)
to pass Butterworth's factory and offices. Join Mill Lane as it runs
off to the right (607558), curving left and skirting the edge of a
boggy wood to reach a lane (606550). Turn right, then left in 100
yards over a stile, through an orchard and over another stile to
cross a stream by stepping stones in the wood beyond. Where the
trees end, keep ahead on a track to reach the hamlet of Yopps Green
at a road (602541) where you turn left.

A farm with three fine conical oasts for hop-drying stands by the road,
and beyond are old half-timbered cottages and the noble gable end of
Little Damas. Tree Lane leads down to the road at Plaxtol and the
parish church (601536), unusual in not being dedicated to any saint,
as it was built in 1649 at the start of Oliver Cromwell's commonwealth
when such idolatry was entirely out of fashion. Light streams through
large windows into the plain interior of the church, whose hammer-
beam roof looks down in dark elegance. In the south transept stands a
carved altar contemporary with the church, on which Moses turns with

upraised staff to watch the Egyptians tumbling off their horses into a billowing Red Sea, while the smiling children of Israel in 17th-century knickerbockers make their way ashore with boxes and bundles on their shoulders.

Return to Yopps Green and turn left just past Little Damas (602540) on a bridleway that climbs over fields and through woods of beech and sweet chestnut to reach the A227 (591540). Cross with care, turning immediately left through a gate along a footpath among trees. In ⅓ mile the path bears right and continues through the woods to a road where you turn left to reach Ightham Mote (584534).

This is one of the National Trust's treasures, a mellow Tudor house that envelops within its stone, brick and timber frame a great hall 200 years older, the whole complex under great chimneys and acres of tiles, surrounded by a moat and set to perfection in its wooded valley. 'A vile and papisticall house' with its priest's holes, Ightham Mote has an equivocal place in Catholic mythology, for it was probably Dame Dorothy Selby of Ightham Mote who wrote the letter to her cousin Lord Mounteagle that exposed the Gunpowder Plot of 1605. She haunts the house in the guise of a Grey Lady, and a skeleton found walled up in a cupboard in the great hall was said to be hers.

Turn right along the road from the entrance to Ightham Mote behind some beautiful 15th-century farm buildings, and in 300 yards turn left opposite One Mote Hill Cottages (582539), climbing the footpath to cross a road (580546) and climb very steeply up Raspit Hill. Go forward 100 yards at the summit and bear right to meet a sunken trackway, where you turn left for 100 yards, then right steeply downhill to cross Ightham Common, pass some ponds and meet the A25 (580556). Turn right along the road (caution – fast traffic!) and in 300 yards turn left by a bus shelter to follow a blue-marked bridleway across the middle of Oldbury Fort.

You can detour here to walk a circuit of Oldbury's ramparts, earth banks smothered in tall oaks and sweet chestnut coppice that enclose the 150 acres of one of Britain's biggest Iron Age forts. Hut circles, grain pits and many artefacts have been uncovered here. Oldbury was built about 100 BC by a native Wealden tribe. The fort was captured by the Belgae and taken from them by the Romans as they marched to London at the start of their invasion in 43 AD.

In ⅓ mile you turn right along the ancient east-west trackway (584564) that bisects the fort, a deeply sunken lane – it was a coach road until the 18th century – that meets a road where you bear right to the A25 by the Cob Tree Inn (592565). Cross the road by

the footbridge into Sevenoaks Road, to turn right uphill on the A227, then in 150 yards left up Mill Lane (594564). In 300 yards take a footpath on the left opposite Mill Lane House, through an orchard. Turn right in 200 yards and bear round to the left to follow a path between a wire fence and a hedge, bending to the right under power lines (600570) to cross a road and continue to Staleys Road in a housing estate. Turn left, then right in 10 yards, up an alleyway beside No. 1. Turn right at the road and immediately left by an oak tree to return to Borough Green railway station.

Penshurst and
the River Medway
(Kent)

INFORMATION

Map OS 1:50,000 Landranger Sheet 188 'Maidstone and the
  Weald of Kent'.
Travel CAR – M25 to Jct 5; A21 to Tonbridge; A26 for 1 mile
  towards Royal Tunbridge Wells; B2176 to Penshurst. Park
  near Penshurst Place.
Length of walk 7 miles – figure-of-eight – start and finish at
  Penshurst Place (✄ *short cut* – 4½ miles).
Conditions Lanes and field paths.
Opening times *Penshurst Place* March–October; house 12–5.30,
  grounds 11–6.
Refreshments Leicester Arms, Penshurst.
Reading Penshurst Place guide book, available at the house.

This is the pastoral face of the River Medway as it winds through
inland Kent, far removed from the great estuary encountered at Lower
Halstow (see Walk No. 35). Here are the celebrated Kentish apple
orchards and hop fields, deeply sunken lanes through rolling countryside and ancient houses scattered along the walk, the most notable
being the 650-year-old Penshurst Place where the Elizabethan man-of-
all-parts Sir Philip Sidney was born.

'A very fair and sportelyke park as any in this parte of England' was the
Steward's description of his master Viscount Lisle's house and grounds
in 1611. Penshurst Place contains the original great hall, built in 1341
for the rich London merchant Sir John de Pulteney, along with his
solar, pantry and buttery, at the heart of the great mansion which has
played host to a roll call of significant names in English history –
among them the Black Prince, Queen Elizabeth I and her favourite the
Earl of Dudley, and the hapless children of King Charles I, whom
Oliver Cromwell dispatched to Penshurst after their father's execution.
  Sir Philip Sidney, the soldier-courtier, musician, poet, politician and
all-round Renaissance man, who gave up a proffered cup of water to a

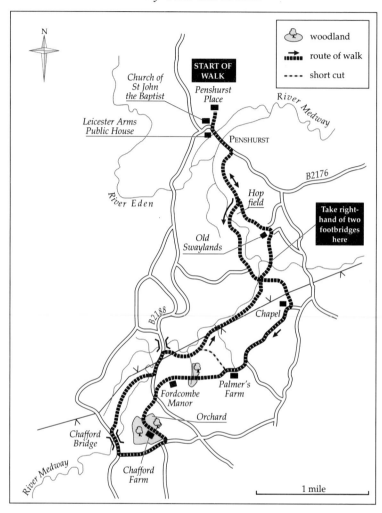

common soldier when both were dying on the field of the Battle of Zutphen in 1586, was born at Penshurst in 1554.

The Jacobean poet and playwright Ben Jonson was impressed with the fishing in the Penshurst ponds:

'. . . If the high swolne Medway faile thy dish
Thou hast thy ponds, that pay thee tribute fish,
Fat, aged carps, that runne into thy net,
And pikes, now weary their owne kinde to eat,
Bright eeles, that emulate them, and leape on land,
Before the fisher, or into his hand.'

After visiting the village full of Tudor houses, and the Church of St John the Baptist with its Sidney monuments, bear right in front of the gates of Penshurst Place (528439) along the B2176, cross two bridges (the second spans the Medway) and in 100 yards turn right along a lane (530435 – 'Poundsgate' sign), with lovely views opening over the Medway valley with its brick and timber farm-houses and conical, white-capped oast houses under wooded hills. In ⅓ mile the path runs along the top of a hop field.

Beer has been the liquid gold of Kent for centuries, particularly the hops that give it that necessary bite. The tall wooden posts in the hop fields are strung with wires and strings by expert pole-climbers, and the hops twine their way upwards along these supports. Weed-clearance is carried out here by grazing sheep. There's a wonderful heady smell from the hops, which the Victorian rural writer Richard Jefferies likened to the dreamy scent of the 'fabled haschish'.

Bear right round the bottom of the hop field to cross the Medway (530427) and recross in ⅓ mile (533421), walking forward and passing through a gate to turn right for ½ mile to a lane on the right (532411 – footpath sign).

Lanes between farming settlements were vital communication routes before cars and tractors came on the scene. Countless boots and animal hooves have trodden this one 10 feet down into the clay over the centuries, walking down to Fordcombe Manor and the waters of the Medway.

(✂ *short cut* – about 250 yards along the lane, and before the end of the farmyard, a path on the right leads down to rejoin the walk on the bank of the Medway.) The lane bears right at the far end of the farmyard of Palmer's Farm (529409), through trees and across a field to cut through a wood (526409) and reach the B2188 below the 16th-century Fordcombe Manor (523409). Turn left up the hill, and right (521406) beside a wooden fence just beyond the entrance to Fordcombe Manor, across a valley over stiles and between fences, turning left across the bottom of an orchard to reach a lane by Chafford Farm (521403). Turn left to the road, then right to cross Chafford Bridge (516402) and turn right to follow the Medway's bank for ½ mile to a footbridge (520409), across which you turn left on the B2188 to a bridge (522413). Go right before the bridge along the Medway's south bank for a mile (✂ *short cut* – rejoins in ⅓ mile), passing a footbridge (533421) and taking the right-hand of two footbridges over a stream (534422). Skirt a hop field, cross a stile and follow the hedge to turn left along a lane (535426) above Old Swaylands.

From Old Swaylands the lane leads back in ¾ mile to the B2176, where you turn left for Penshurst.

The Wealden clay is rich in nuggets of iron, and from Roman times the great forest of the Weald was felled for charcoal to fire the iron furnaces of the area. Old Swaylands, a beautiful old timbered house of crooked angles under ancient red tiles, was once the home of one of the wealthy Kentish ironmasters. The central section of the house belongs to the early Middle Ages, when Kent's wealth and influence were at their height.

Godstone Station, Blindley Heath and Crowhurst
(Surrey)

INFORMATION

Map OS 1:50,000 Landranger Sheet 187 'Dorking, Reigate and Crawley'.

Travel

TRAIN (BR) – Godstone.

CAR – M25 to Jct 6; A22 towards East Grinstead; park at Godstone station (3 miles).

BUS – Green Line (Victoria) 081 668–7261. Local information: 081 541–9639. BR to West Croydon station; bus from West Croydon bus station (next to BR station) stops at Godstone BR station.

Length of walk 7½ miles – circular – start and finish at Godstone station.

Conditions Field paths and green lanes; two short stretches of A22, on pavement.

Refreshments The Railway, South Godstone (opposite station); Farmhouse Table pub, Blindley Heath.

Reading Booklets on Crowhurst church and parish, available in church.

Quiet footpaths lead you through the pasture of south-east Surrey past the superb Tudor manor house of Crowhurst Place, and the little church at Crowhurst where a mighty ancient yew tree stands in the churchyard. At Blindley Heath there are memories of the bare-knuckle prize fights of bygone days, and at Ardenrun estate of a celebrated motor-racing driver of the 1920s and 30s.

From the approach road to Godstone station (368484) turn left on to the A22, and in 10 yards left down a tarmac path opposite The Railway pub, which runs through a housing estate to the right of No. 95 and follows the railway line to a road (355485). Turn left under the railway, and in 300 yards left down a track (356481 – concrete footpath sign) to meet the A22, where you turn right

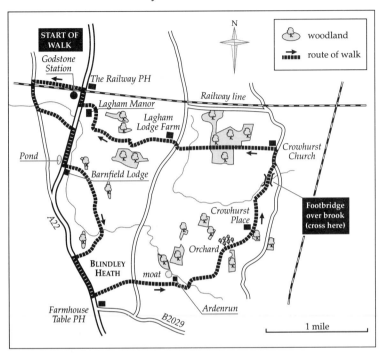

along the pavement (361478) for a traffic-laden ¼ mile. Beside a pond, cross the road with care (360473) and walk past Barnfield Lodge down a lane. Where it bends sharp right (363471) keep straight on and ahead again at a crossroads of paths (364468) to turn left along the A22 through Blindley Heath (361460).

In the late 18th and early 19th century the fashionable young sporting bloods of London who called themselves the 'Corinthians' would flock in their carriages to Blindley Heath, to mingle with huge crowds of working folk assembled to watch illegal bare-knuckle fights between such heroes as Hickman the Gas-Light Man and his opponent Oliver. This pair fought 10 rounds in 13 minutes here in 1821 – each round ended when one man was knocked down, so this was a particularly bloody contest. Blindley Heath was a favourite venue because of its location a few miles from the Kent and Sussex borders – if the law were rumoured to be approaching, the combatants and their backers could quickly escape.

Just before the Farmhouse Table pub, turn left (363455) and follow the path across the fields; it becomes a lane that meets a road (370457), which you cross to walk down the drive of Ardenrun estate.

The stable block with its gilt clock and bell turret (376457) once served the neo-Georgian pile of Ardenrun, built in 1906 for Woolf Barnato, the son of a South African diamond magnate. Barnato became a famous motor-racing driver, wining the prestigious Le Mans 24-hour race. His great house was burned to the ground in 1933, but fine buildings of the estate can still be seen.

Follow the drive as it bends left around a pond, and in 30 yards turn right through a kissing gate along a grassy track. In 300 yards turn left over a stile (381457) and up two fields to turn right over a stile (382461 – yellow arrow). Skirt an orchard and follow the yellow arrows to the driveway of Crowhurst Place (388464).

Crowhurst Place is the archetype of a moated Tudor manor, with half-timbered walls infilled with brick and whitewashed plaster, tiny latticed window, every conceivable angle of gable, chimney, roof and dormer and white fantail pigeons nestling on the roof tiles. Its restoration early this century was cleverly carried out to blend with the original portions of the building. This was the home of the influential Gaynesford family for centuries; the stories say that King Henry VIII often stayed in the house on his way to dally with Anne Boleyn at Hever Castle.

Cross the drive and walk across fields; don't cross the brook when you reach it (388468), but turn right to follow it to another footbridge (390470), which you cross to reach the road (390472) and Crowhurst church (390475).

Opposite the church gate stands the Tudor, red brick Mansion House of the Angell family. At the east end of the church, a yew tree 11 yards round and said to be 1500 years old raises fantastically gnarled branches from a split and hollow trunk, into which in 1820 a Crowhurst publican inserted a door and a bench to seat 14 people. In the 1850s the church authorities put an end to the traditional Palm Sunday fair held under the yew's mighty canopy – it had become a drinker's orgy.

Parts of the church date back 800 years – only half the age of the yew! Behind the altar are pre-Raphaelite mosaic paintings, and an east window with medieval glass featuring feathery angels and multiple panes showing a girl holding out a garland of flowers – her mane of hair makes her look like Alice in Wonderland. Half-hidden under the south end of the altar is a fine tomb slab to Anne Forster (1591), the daughter of Thomas Gaynesford of Crowhurst Place. Anne's children kneel piously each side, and the object in the middle, like a bundle of straw, is Anne herself, tied up head and foot in her winding sheet. The slab is of solid iron – all this part of the Surrey Weald was engaged in those days in the mining, smelting and working of iron.

Leave the churchyard through a kissing gate on the west side and follow yellow arrows for a mile across fields and through a wood to a road (376475). Turn right, and in 30 yards left (footpath fingerpost). Pass Lagham Lodge Farm into a green lane that becomes a track curving across the fields. Thirty yards beyond a sharp left-hand bend, turn left between wire fences (370477 – blue arrow) and follow the blue arrows round the weedy, tree-smothered moat of 17th-century Lagham Manor to the A22 (362481), where you turn right to Godstone station.

42

Woldingham, Marden Park
and the Pilgrims' Way
(Surrey)

INFORMATION

Map OS 1:50,000 Landranger Sheet 187 'Dorking, Reigate and
   Crawley'.
Travel
   TRAIN (BR) – Woldingham.
   CAR – M25 to Jct 6; A22 towards London; at 1st round-
      about (3 miles), last exit on right to Woldingham station
      (1½ miles). Park at station.
Length of walk 6 miles – circular – start and finish at
   Woldingham station.
Conditions Farm lanes, woodland and field paths. Some
   woodland paths are steep and muddy.
Refreshments White Lion, Warlingham (358585 – 1½ miles
   north of Woldingham station).

Marden Park, a magnificent Victorian red-brick pile in neo-Jacobean
style, sits handsomely in its secluded valley as a focus for this ramble
around the north Surrey downs. Beautiful woods, remote farms straddling high ridges and a stretch of the historic Pilgrims' Way are other
tempting features of the walk.

**Arriving at Woldingham station (360562), cross the line by the
footbridge and go through a doorway by the waiting room. Walk
down the path to turn left beside the 'cottage orné' lodge along the
roadway through the lovely Marden valley. Pass the drive to Marden
Park Farm (360558) and walk through the gates of Marden Park at
Middle Lodge (360549) with its 12-foot chimney. Marden Park
(360548) lies just around the curve of the drive.**

Behind a thick yew hedge stands the imposing mansion of Marden
Park, built in the 1880s in splendid style – curly Jacobean gables, rows
of windows, enough roof area to shelter an army, beautifully kept
grounds with square-clipped hedges, classically laid out gardens and a

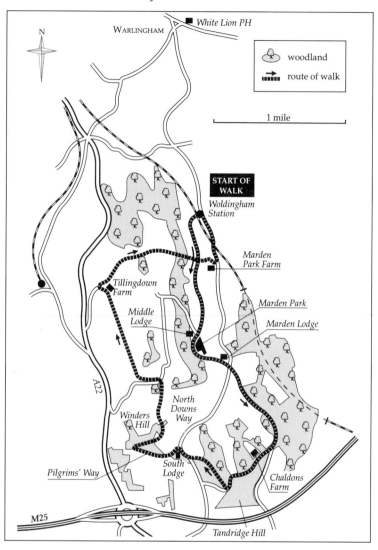

whole arboretum of trees. Marden Park as it stands today houses the Convent of the Sacred Heart, its grounds dotted with the buildings of a girls' school. The house replaced a mansion built in the 1670s by Sir Robert Clayton, 'the wealthiest merchant in London', on the site of the medieval village of Marden which had been abandoned after the Black Death catastrophe of 1348/9. John Evelyn, the diarist, visited Marden Park in October 1677, shortly after it was built, and recorded: 'It is in such solitude among hills as, being not above 16 miles from London, seems almost incredible, the ways up to it are so winding and intricate.'

Looking down on Marden Park from the hillside beyond, you get a good idea of the house's solitude as it stands over its sweep of lawns among the trees, dwarfed by the high sides of the dry chalk valley that enfolds it.

Pass the house, and bear left in front of the gates at Marden Lodge (363546); then in 50 yards right over a stile (wooden footpath fingerpost) and up the hill, to look back over Marden Park. Go over a stile and into woods (365544), bearing right in ¼ mile in a clearing and descending to join a track and then meet the road (369536), where you turn right.

This is a lovely spot, with the National Trust's Hanging Woods on the escarpment of Tandridge Hill on your left, and Chaldons Farm, red brick and knapped flint set in a perfect cottage garden, on the right. Just past the farm are some tremendous old oaks, swollen and bulbous, most of their limbs shed over the centuries, but still gamely sprouting leaves year after year.

Go down the steep hill to turn right on the North Downs Way (363532 – NDW sign and yellow arrow), and walk through trees and down a spine of hill to South Lodge (358536), where you follow the ancient Pilgrims' Way under huge beech and yew trees above a vineyard. Just beyond some cottages a North Downs Way sign points left (352536); turn right here (footpath sign) to climb the steep steps up through the woods on Winders Hill. Turn left at the top over a stile under huge, gnarled beech trees; in 400 yards the path forks at an immense fallen tree trunk (356538), and here you turn left over a stile and across a field to turn right along the hedge to an old green footpath sign. Keep ahead to turn left on a farm track (356544) and walk for a glorious upland mile between old hedges towards Tillingdown Farm.

In his book *Nature Near London* (1883) the great 19th-century rural writer Richard Jefferies described the farm workers of these downs, within sight of London but a world apart from it:

> 'When the plough pauses the ploughman looks over the low cropped hedge and sees far off the glitter of the sunshine on the glass roof of the Crystal Palace. But though hard by, he is not of London. The horses go on again, and his gaze is bent down upon the furrow.
> '. . . Suddenly there comes a hollow booming sound – the big guns at Woolwich are at work. The shepherd takes no heed – neither he nor his sheep. His ears must acknowledge the sound, but his mind pays no attention. He knows of nothing but his sheep.'

The track swings left (349554) to curve to the right round Tillingdown Farm; pass in front of the farmhouse and keep forward through a gateway, then bear left over a gate and follow a yellow arrow down to the right to cross the bottom of a valley (351558) beside a fence. Climb the opposite slope to cross a stile at the left-hand corner of a wood, and follow the fence over the crest of the ridge and steeply down through woods into the Marden valley. Cross the road (360558) and go up the drive of Marden Park Farm, passing between an old flint barn and a row of estate cottages to turn left along a rough road (362558). Cross the railway and turn left to reach Woldingham station.

43

Chipstead
and the North Downs
(Surrey)

INFORMATION

Map OS 1:50,000 Landranger Sheet 187 'Dorking, Reigate and
   Crawley'.
Travel
   TRAIN (BR) – Chipstead.
   CAR – M25 to Jct 8; A217 towards Banstead; in 3 miles,
      B2032 to Chipstead. Park at railway station.
Length of walk 6½ miles – circular – start and finish at
   Chipstead station.
Conditions Field and woodland paths, country roads.
Refreshments White Hart, near Elmore Road crossroads
   (279571).

The steep-sided valleys south of Chipstead are surprisingly quiet and
peaceful, hemmed in as they are by major roads and motorways. Here
you can stroll among fields and woods unfrequented by ramblers, with
good views over the rolling, wooded north Surrey landscape – carefully
conserved downland countryside, deservedly so: a little green haven
between the roaring roads.

Chipstead is in Surrey only by the skin of its teeth – London's fringes
are three miles to the north. When the railway arrived in 1897 the
sleepy hamlet grew apace, sprouting desirable residences on its hillside
and around the railway station. These days it's a popular commuter
village, with a classic line of early 20th-century half-timbered shops
(including a Tandoori restaurant and an 'architectural miniaturist')
flanking the road to the station, and neat villas peeping out among the
trees. The Chipstead Players put on plays in their newly-built theatre
to add spice to the comfortable not-quite-suburban life of the village.

**Turn left out of the station (277583), and left again above the
shops in Station Approach (bridleway sign) to cross the railway and
climb a steep path with steps past Chipstead Golf Club's clubhouse**

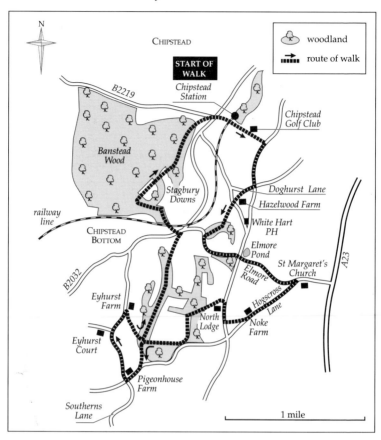

**(the bar is labelled '19th Hole') and over the fairways to turn right
at the road (280580) for 400 yards to the crossroads. Turn right
here along Doghurst Lane, and in 200 yards left (279574 – footpath sign) through the gates of Tara Park. Bear right round
Hazelwood Farm between iron pillars to cross a road over a stile;
follow the fence on your right into woodland and down to turn left
along a lane (273570) and climb to the crossroads by rushy Elmore
Pond (278568). (The White Hart is 150 yards to the left here.)
Cross into Elmore Road to reach St Margaret's Church on its triangular green (283564) where a splendid Turkey oak stands.**

The stubby 13th-century tower of St Margaret's stands over a Norman
nave, a round-arched Norman north doorway and an ornate, crum-
bling west doorway. There's some fine medieval glass in the east
window and in the south transept, and a 15th-century screen.
Chipstead has named its village hall after its former vicar, the Reverend

Peter Aubertin, who was architect, fund-raiser and glass-painter during the church's 19th-century restoration.

From the church, pass the war memorial and walk up Hogscross Lane. Pass Noke Farm and in 100 yards turn right over a stile (278560 – footpath sign and yellow arrow) through rhododendron woods to turn right along the road and in 200 yards left by North Lodge along a well-surfaced lane (277563 – footpath sign). In ¼ mile where the lane swings right, go sharp left (271561 – yellow arrow) across the slope of a field.

At the road turn right (271558) and in 50 yards keep forward (wooden footpath sign) along a grassy path that climbs through woodland. Bear left at a post (yellow arrow), and in 50 yards left again at a crossroads of paths (post with four yellow arrows); 50 yards on, go right (yellow arrow) to drop to the road by crooked old Pigeonhouse Farm (266554). Turn right, and in 150 yards right again opposite Southerns Lane up an old track that passes between large and ugly Eyhurst Court and a handsome flint house with a portico. Bear right past the house (263560), right again in front of Eyhurst Farm through a gate (yellow arrow), and follow a fence on your right, over stiles and into a wood, where in 30 yards you turn left at a post (yellow arrow) to walk for ¾ mile through the trees.

These old woods of oak, ash, beech and yew still show scars from the great gale of 16th October 1987. Trunks snapped clean off, uprooted beeches, shattered yew groves – all bear witness to the devastating force of the terrific hurricane which flayed the south of England.

Cross the B2032 at Chipstead Bottom (271570) and follow a footpath sign opposite to cross the railway into Banstead Wood. In 200 yards where the path forks, bear right; in 250 yards turn left at a T-junction of paths and keep right uphill to reach wooden posts on your right (263573). Turn right in front of them and continue for a mile along the edge of the wood.

The open grassland of Stagbury Downs, to your right as you walk, is herb-rich chalk downland sward. The sheep that used to graze these downs (and flavour their meat on the mint that grew here) have gone from the Surrey landscape, and the sward of Stagbury Downs is being steadily invaded by scrub of coarse grass, dogwood, buckthorn and hawthorn. Now a project is under way to clear some of the scrub and reintroduce sheep to graze it back to the traditional sward – Herdwick and Jacob sheep, good browsing hill species that can thrive on a mixture of vegetation. Patches of scrub are being retained for the variety of wildlife they shelter.

Keep the line of the path to turn downhill and enter the trees
(270578); bear left on joining another path here to reach the
B2219 (273583). Turn right, left at the crossroads along Outwood
Lane and in 20 yards right up Station Approach to Chipstead
station.

·44·

Leigh
and Reigate
(Surrey)

INFORMATION

Map OS 1:50,000 Landranger Sheet 187 'Dorking, Reigate and Crawley'.

Travel

    CAR – M25 to Jct 8; A217 through Reigate towards Crawley; at junction of A217 and A2044, turn right on minor road, then in 2½ miles turn left for Leigh. Park on green near Plough Inn.

    BUS – Green Line (Victoria) 081 668–7261. Local information: 081 541–9639. London Victoria–Kingston–Reigate bus garage in Lesbourne Road, ½ mile from Park Hill (see map – start and finish walk here); or BR to Dorking station, bus to Leigh village green.

Length of walk 6 miles – circular – start and finish at Plough Inn, Leigh

Conditions Field paths, some muddy.

Refreshments Plough Inn, Leigh.

From the attractive village of Leigh around its green, you walk on well-marked paths through the rich farmland of eastern Surrey, with the rampart of the North Downs always in view to the north. There are memories of the ironworking industries that both scarred and enriched what is now pleasant pastureland, and a climb up to a high ridge overlooking Reigate and the farmlands to the south.

Leigh takes its name – and its pronunciation, 'Lye' – from the Saxon word for a forest clearing. When the village was created in medieval times, the whole area was covered in the original wildwood that had been growing since before the Stone Age. Leigh had an ironworks from Tudor times onwards, and the forest was quickly reduced to a scattering of copses as the trees were felled to create farmland and to fuel the iron furnaces.

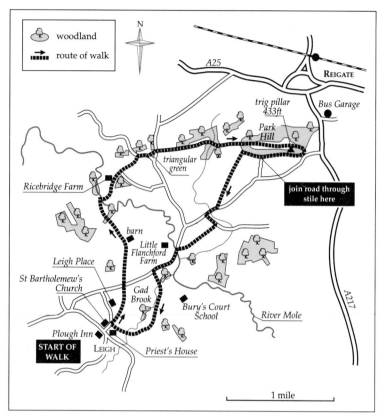

woodland
route of walk

N

A25
REIGATE
Bus Garage
trig pillar
433ft
Park
Hill
triangular
green
join road through
stile here
Ricebridge Farm
barn
Little
Flanchford
Farm
Leigh Place
St Bartholemew's
Church
Gad
Brook
Bury's Court
School
River Mole
A217
Plough Inn
START OF
WALK
LEIGH
Priest's House

1 mile

The village stands round a broad, tree-lined green. Parts of the weatherboarded Plough Inn date back 600 years, as does the long, half-timbered medieval Priest's House opposite. Between them stands the pump of the village well under a handsome wooden canopy – the well was the *raison d'être* of Leigh, since in this dry plain of Wealden clay no settlement could properly establish itself until a well had been sunk to reach the water-bearing chalk, scores of feet below the ground.

Next to the Priest's House stands the tall broach spire and massively heavy stone roof of the 15th-century Church of St Bartholomew, thoroughly restored in Victorian times, with a simple, barn-like interior which contains some notable Victorian stained glass. In the 'Suffer little children to come unto me' window in the north wall are strong-faced men and women with stern chins and noses, one woman with flowing pre-Raphaelite hair under an embroidered cap. The chancel has the four evangelists with life-like faces, and a brilliantly coloured and shaded east window Crucifixion by Kempe.

Leave the lych gate on the north side of the church (224470), turn right and in 100 yards right through a kissing gate. Bear right and walk round two sides of the field edge to the diagonally opposite corner, with a view to your left of the bell turret and many-windowed walls of Leigh Place (225473).

The Gothic windows and turret of Leigh Place date only from 1810, but parts of the moated old house are more than 800 years old. It contains a priest's hole as witness to the religious sympathies of the inhabitants after the Reformation, and the ghost of a White Lady.

A yellow arrow directs you to cross a stream and reach the road (227475), from which a deeply rutted track runs north across the fields. Before a barn, bear diagonally left (227481 – yellow arrow) to a stile in the hedge opposite (yellow arrow). Cross a field, and the muddy Gad Brook (224485), then the next field to turn right in the corner and cross the River Mole (223487).

The Mole has been called 'sulky and sullen', and looking down at its murky waters you can see why. There's little here to connect this slug-gish waterway with the broad river that slices through the North Downs near Dorking to reach the River Thames.

Turn immediately left over a stile and cross a field to another stile and a lane skirting Ricebridge Farm beneath a wonderful tree-house high in an old oak that looks just like Dorothy's flying house in the *Wizard of Oz* film. In 200 yards where the lane bends right (226491) go forward over stiles on a field path to turn right on a road (229494). Bear left at a triangular green, and cross a T-junc-tion (231494) on to a well-marked path through the fields that reaches another road (239495). Here a bridleway sign points along a tarmac path that climbs in ⅓ mile to the road under the ridge of Park Hill (243495).
Cross the road and climb up steps, then straight up the side of Park Hill to walk along the ridge to a trig pillar (251494 – 433 ft).

This high, open spine of land, surrounded by Scots pine, silver birch and oak, was given to Reigate Corporation in 1920 'for the use and quiet enjoyment of the public'. You can see both North and South Downs from its heights, as well as the scattered houses of Reigate lying under the North Downs.

Descend beyond the trig pillar, turning right at the bottom on a path that skirts back along the foot of Park Hill. In ⅓ mile go through a stile to turn right along the road (246493); then in 250 yards go left (244494 – footpath sign) across a field to join a lane that curves left. In 100 yards turn right (footpath sign) across two fields to a road (240486). Turn right, and left at a T-junction, then in 150 yards go right (240483) across a field and down a track. At the end, aim half-way down the left-hand hedge to join a lane and turn right to reach a road (234480).

Turn left to cross the River Mole and pass Little Flanchford Farm and the drive to Bury's Court School. In 150 yards, opposite a letter box (231477), go left on a footpath between a fence and a hedge to cross a stream and turn right along its bank. Cross a stile and a field, aiming well to the right of the central electricity pole for a stile in the hedge. Cross this and turn right, then go through a gate, and keep a fence on your right to descend and cross a stream (227469) and the following field to a stile and a path to Leigh churchyard.

45

Gomshall, the Abingers
and Leith Hill
(Surrey)

INFORMATION

Map OS 1:50,000 Landranger Sheet 187 'Dorking, Reigate and Crawley'.
Travel
  TRAIN (BR) – Gomshall.
  CAR – M25 to Jct 9; A24 to Dorking; A25 towards Guildford. Park near Gomshall station (6 miles).
  BUS – Green Line (Victoria) 081 668–7261. Local information: 081 541–9639. London Victoria Guildford–Gomshall; bus stops at The Compasses pub, on A25 ¼ mile before Gomshall BR station.
Length of walk 11½ miles – circular – start and finish at Gomshall station (✂ *short cut* – 8 miles).
Conditions Field and woodland paths, lanes. Muddy in the woods.
Opening times
  Leith Hill Tower Fine weekends and Bank Holidays, 11–3.
  Church of St John the Evangelist, Wotton – Sunday afternoons in summer. Key details in porch.
Refreshments Frog Island Vegetarian Restaurant, Gomshall; The Volunteer, Sutton; Abinger Hatch Inn; Wotton Hatch Inn, Wotton.

You'll be well muddied and well satisfied at the end of this longish walk through the thickly wooded, rolling Surrey countryside, overlooked by the escarpment of the North Downs and studded with ponds that once powered the Weald's iron industry. Beautiful woodland leads to a famous Surrey viewpoint, and to some of the quietest and loneliest hollows and valleys within an hour of London.

From Gomshall station (089478) cross the A25 and walk through

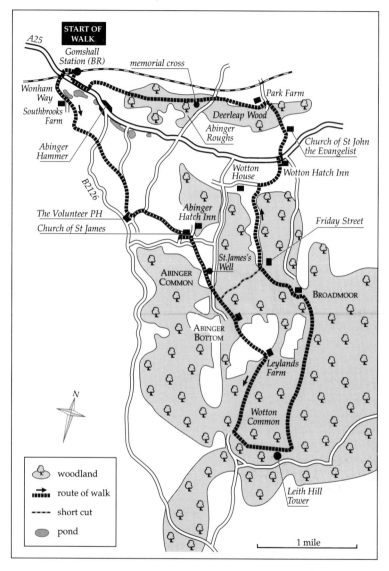

START OF WALK

A25

Gomshall Station (BR)

memorial cross

Wonham Way

Southbrooks Farm

Park Farm

Deerleap Wood

Abinger Roughs

Abinger Hammer

Church of St John the Evangelist

B2126

Wotton House

Wotton Hatch Inn

The Volunteer PH

Church of St James

Abinger Hatch Inn

Friday Street

St James's Well

ABINGER COMMON

BROADMOOR

ABINGER BOTTOM

Leylands Farm

N

Wotton Common

🌳 woodland

route of walk

short cut

pond

Leith Hill Tower

1 mile

the pedestrian tunnel under the railway to turn right down Wonham Way.

The sedgy woodland here hides the remains of some of the many hammer ponds you'll encounter along the walk. From the late 14th century they were dug and flooded to power the drop-hammers that shaped the pig iron of the Wealden ironworking trade, which flourished on local wood, iron ore and water until the mighty ironworks of northern England stole the business in the 17th and 18th centuries.

On a right-hand bend (089474) turn left past Southbrooks Farm, and immediately right; a clear path runs beside the hedge here, but instead take the path to the right, diagonally across a field. Bear right into a sunken lane, and in 300 yards go over a stile on the left (092470), keeping ahead into a sunken lane which descends to cross the B2126 (096469). Cross a stile and footbridge, climbing a slope to cross two fields diagonally. Descend with a hedge on your left to enter another sunken lane which joins a track (103464) and reaches a hollow lane (105460). (The Volunteer pub is 30 yards to your right.) Turn left up the lane, and in 150 yards right up steep steps; turn left over a stile at the top, then right through a gate and along a farm lane and a green path to reach Abinger Hatch between the church and the manor house (115459).

The Norman Church of St James, barn-like inside and plainly restored, contains some beautiful 15th-century English relief panels of alabaster, delicately carved – a Crucifixion in the south porch with a four-winged angel offering the Holy Grail at the foot of the cross, a moustachio'd knight in medieval armour and St John in a big, baggy hat; by the font a splendid beheading of John the Baptist.

The red brick, tile-hung manor house opposite was built in the 1680s by the powerful local Evelyn family. There's a moated Norman motte near the path, and elsewhere in the grounds a Mesolithic pit dwelling three feet deep and 15 feet across, where more than 1,000 worked flints were found during excavations.

Across the road stands the old Abinger Hatch Inn; and ½ mile along to the right, on Abinger Common's village green, the gabled and pillared covering over St James's Well, its Victorian lifting mechanism of cogs and fly wheel (an Evelyn gift to the villagers in 1893) still intact.

Turn right from the Abinger Hatch Inn to Abinger Common's village green (120455), bear right ('Leith Hill' sign) and in 75 yards left ('Abinger Bottom' sign) (✂ *short cut* – opposite Fir Cottage a bridleway runs off to the left for ½ mile to rejoin the walk at Friday Street). Turn right just past Fir Cottage (123452 – footpath finger-post) through woods, keeping ahead to descend to the huddle of cottages at Abinger Bottom (127448). Bear uphill ('No Through Road' sign) past the Old Bake House and Longfield Farm, to the top of the trees; turn left (yellow arrow) round a field edge, then left over a stile (yellow arrow) to a road (133446). Turn right past Leylands Farm, and in 200 yards left through a wooden barrier on to a clear path through the woods of Wotton Common for a mile. The path descends to meet a well-marked bridleway; turn left and follow it up, forking left to reach Leith Hill Tower (139431).

This is the highest point in Surrey at nearly 1,000 feet, a greensand ridge with a mighty view to London and over a great stretch of Wealden woods and farmlands. Richard Hull lies buried under the floor of the brick-and-ironstone tower he built in 1766.

The woods of Wotton Common and Leith Hill (oak, silver birch, beech, pine, fir) contain many of the trees planted here by the celebrated 17th-century diarist John Evelyn of Wotton House – he was an early conservationist, very indignant about the 'impolitick diminution of our Timber', which was then being felled in enormous quantities for ship-building and iron-smelting.

Pass the tower, descending steeply to a saddle of ground (141432) and turn left before a National Trust 'Duke's Warren' sign down a wide trackway (blue 'GW' bridleway arrow) which runs north through beautifully quiet, wooded heathland for a mile to pass some cottages deep in the trees and reach the road at Broadmoor (136457). Turn left, then in 150 yards right beyond Leith Cottage, bending to the right; in 70 yards take a sunken track to the left (134457) that climbs to continue ahead over two roads and drops steeply beside the ancient boundary bank of Severell's Copse to the pond and road at Friday Street (129458) (✄ *short cut* – rejoins here). Turn left, then right in 50 yards (footpath fingerpost) on a path that skirts the long ponds of Wotton estate, with a good view of the big red pile of Wotton House (122470). Turn right at the lane to cross the A25 beside the Wotton Hatch Inn (126476) and make for the squat tower, partly Saxon, of the Church of St John the Evangelist (126480).

Cross a stile by the church gate and bear left round a field edge and through a wood to reach Park Farm (121484).

This secluded valley, dominated by the sombre green wall of the North Downs, is blessedly roadless, utterly quiet and peaceful, disturbed only by the clack of the occasional train. What a pleasure it is to walk here.

Pass between barns and follow blue bridleway arrows along the bottom of Deerleap Wood to reach a road (112482). Turn left, and in 15 yards right (bridleway fingerpost) through the woodland and commons of Abinger Roughs, to pass a large memorial cross (110481).

The cross marks the spot where, on 19th July 1873, the Bishop of Winchester, Samuel Wilberforce, was killed in a fall from his horse. Bishop Wilberforce was the son of the great slavery reformer, William Wilberforce.

Keep inside the trees, following a straight line over open commons and through belts of woodland, across a tarmac road (096478) and through a final piece of woodland. Where this ends, bear left (092478) to turn right along the A25 back to Gomshall station.

46

Gomshall, Pilgrims' Way
and Box Hill
(Surrey)

INFORMATION

Map OS 1:50,000 Landranger Sheet 187 'Dorking, Reigate and Crawley'.

Travel

    TRAIN (BR) – Gomshall.

    CAR – M25 to Jct 9; A24 to Dorking; A25 towards Guildford. Park near Gomshall station (6 miles).

    BUS – Green Line (Victoria) 081 668–7261. Local information: 081 541–9639. Outward journey as walk No. 45. Return: Burford Bridge Hotel – Kingston–London Victoria.

Length of walk 10 miles – linear. Return by train from Boxhill and Westhumble station: change at Dorking, walking from Dorking North station to Dorking Deepdene station (2 mins) to catch Gomshall train (✂ *short cut* – 8 miles).

Conditions Woodland tracks – can be very muddy. Walking boots essential. Very steep climb up Box Hill, and steep, slippery descent – worth it for the view, but after nine miles you may not have the puff!

Refreshments White Horse, Shere; Stepping Stones, Westhumble; Burford Bridge Hotel.

Reading *A Guide to the Pilgrims' Way and North Downs Way* by Christopher John Wright (Constable).

This walk offers you a glimpse of Shere, 'the prettiest village in Surrey', a long stretch of exhilarating high-level walking on the crest of the North Downs escarpment, stretches of forgotten old roads deep in the beech woods and a final knee-cracking climb up Box Hill to one of the classic views of England.

(✂ *Short cut* – from Gomshall station turn left along the A25 for 250 yards, then left up a lane to rejoin the walk where it leaves the North Downs Way on Hackhurst Downs.) From Gomshall station

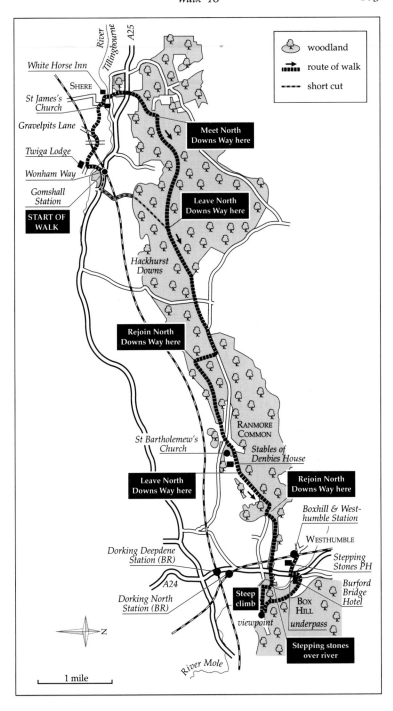

White Horse Inn

SHERE

St James's Church

Gravelpits Lane

Twiga Lodge

Wonham Way

Gomshall Station

START OF WALK

River Tillingbourne

A25

Meet North Downs Way here

Leave North Downs Way here

Hackhurst Downs

Rejoin North Downs Way here

RANMORE COMMON

St Bartholemew's Church

Stables of Denbies House

Leave North Downs Way here

Rejoin North Downs Way here

Boxhill & Westhumble Station

WESTHUMBLE

Stepping Stones PH

Dorking Deepdene Station (BR)

A24

Dorking North Station (BR)

Burford Bridge Hotel

Steep climb

BOX HILL

underpass

viewpoint

Stepping stones over river

River Mole

N

woodland

route of walk

short cut

1 mile

**(089478) cross the A25 and go through the pedestrian tunnel
under the railway to turn right down Wonham Way. At the left-
hand bend by Twiga Lodge (087475) turn right, then right again
under the railway, turning left here to a crossroads (082476). Cross
into Gravelpits Lane, and in 100 yards go right by Gravel Pits
Farmhouse into a lane which crosses fields. In ½ mile turn right
through a gate (075477) onto the path to St James's Church in
Shere (074478).**

This is a wonderful Norman church, full of treasures and kept
unlocked. The south doorway and tower are Norman; the 13th-
century west doorway is tall and graceful. Inside, there's 14th-century
glass, a massive oak Crusader chest 800 years old, some fine medieval
brasses and a beautiful little bronze statue of the Madonna and Child,
only two inches high but superbly detailed, which was unearthed from
a bramble bush by a dog – it probably belonged to a pilgrim going to
Canterbury along the nearby Pilgrims' Way. A little quatrefoil window
and a squint slit in the chancel, together with traces of a doorway in
the north wall, show the site of the tiny cell where the Anchoress of
Shere, Christine Carpenter, was immured by her own wish in 1329.
Evidently this solitary confinement undertaken for the Lord proved too
much for Christine – displayed near her little windows are copies of the
letter she wrote to the Bishop of Winchester in 1332 begging to be
allowed back into her cell, and the Bishop's agreement with the proviso
that she would not be allowed to 'wander from the laudable intention
otherwise solemnly undertaken and again run about, being torn to
pieces by attacks of the Tempter, which Heaven forbid.'

**Turn right opposite the White Horse pub, left at the T-junction
(073479) and right up a track beside the recreation ground, which
goes under the A25 and bears right to climb the escarpment for ½
mile to its junction with the North Downs Way on top of the ridge
(077489). Turn right and follow National Trust acorn symbols.**

The North Downs Way follows the course of the ancient Pilgrims' Way
from Winchester to the tomb of St Thomas à Becket at Canterbury.
The track has been in use for thousands of years, taking travellers on a
high-level route that kept them clear of the dangers in the thickly
wooded, swampy valley bottoms. There are far-flung views between the
beech and yew trees up here, south across the ridges and forests of the
Weald.

**In 1½ miles the path reaches Hackhurst Downs, where the North
Downs Way runs downhill to the right (101491) (✂ *short cut* joins
walk here), but keep ahead (wooden post with purple ring) for just
over a mile.**

Suddenly the track sheds its character of a well-used long-distance ramblers' footpath, and becomes darker, dirtier and more mysterious. It runs through thickets of holly and yew; then, where the trees open out, along the edge of unfrequented beech woods – a rutted old road, gleaming with pools of rainwater, used only by off-road motoring fanatics. Its ancient boundary banks are knitted together by fantastically distorted beech pollards. Here you recapture a little of both the discomfort and the excitement of pre-tarmac roads.

Join the road at Dogkennel Green (120500); pass a turning on the left and in 150 yards go right on a bridleway (126501) which soon joins a surfaced roadway. You cross a track and descend through a conifer plantation to turn left at wooden barriers along the North Downs Way (127497 – National Trust acorn symbol) for a long mile to the road at Ranmore Common (142503). Turn right, then left to pass St Bartholomew's, the 'Church on the North Downs Way'.

The flint-cobble church, elegant inside and out, was designed by the eminent Victorian architect Sir George Gilbert Scott for Lord Ashcombe of Denbies House, son of Thomas Cubitt who was responsible for building much of 19th-century London. The church, and the school built next door to it, became the focus of the Denbies estate – everyone had to attend.

Pass St Bartholomew's Church, and then the imposing Denbies stable block – the great house was pulled down in 1954 – and keep ahead up a driveway where the road bends left (151506). A North Downs Way fingerpost points to the right, but continue along the drive and into the woodland beyond, descending to turn right (158513 – blue arrow) and drop downhill to turn left along the North Downs Way (159512). Follow the path under the railway (168513) and cross the A25 – either with a dangerous sprint, or by turning left and using the underpass. Take the path opposite (National Trust 'Box Hill Stepping Stones' sign), cross the River Mole by the stepping stones (173513) and turn right to start a very steep climb up the face of Box Hill.

Wild box trees are rare in Britain, but you'll see their thin trunks and shiny, oval leaves growing with the knobbled old yews among the tangle of brambles and old-man's-beard on Box Hill's steep, chalky escarpment. The view from the 600-foot summit – the wide-rolling Weald, the South Downs, the dark bar of Ashdown Forest, the promontory of Leith Hill – is not soon forgotten.

At the top of the climb go right for a few yards to enjoy the view (179151); then turn back on the path that runs along the edge of

the escarpment all the way down the broad shoulder of Box Hill to the Burford Bridge Hotel at the foot of the hill (172519).

These days a plush place, the Burford Bridge Hotel (formerly the Fox and Hounds) was newly built when Admiral Horatio Nelson in 1805 spent his last night in England here with Emma Hamilton, before setting sail for the Battle of Trafalgar and his own death. Among other famous residents was John Keats, who stayed at the hotel in the winter of 1817 and climbed Box Hill by moonlight to receive inspiration for his masterpiece 'Endymion':

> '. . . Under the brow
> Of some steep mossy hill, where ivy dun
> Would hide us up, although spring leaves were more;
> And where dark yew-trees, as we rustle through,
> Will drop their scarlet-berry cups of dew!
> O thou wouldst joy to live in such a place! . . .
> For by one step the blue sky shouldst thou find,
> And by another, in deep dell below,
> See, through the trees, a little river go . . .'

From the hotel walk left along the A25 to cross it by the subway and go up Westhumble Street. Pass the Stepping Stones pub to find Boxhill and Westhumble station on the left (168519); here you catch your train to Dorking North station, walk a few yards to Dorking Deepdene station, and entrain for Gomshall station.

47

Ashtead and Epsom Commons, and the Epsom Well
(Surrey)

INFORMATION

Map OS 1:50,000 Landranger Sheet 187 'Dorking, Reigate and Crawley'.

Travel

TRAIN (BR) – Ashtead.

CAR – M25 to Jct 9; A24 towards Epsom; in 1 mile, turn left in Ashtead at 'library' sign to find station ¾ mile along road. Park at station.

BUS – Green Line (Victoria) 081 668–7261. Local information: 081 541–9639. London Victoria–Kingston–Ashtead Pond (200 yards from Ashtead BR station – see map).

Length of walk 4 miles – circular – start and finish at Ashtead station.

Conditions Paths over commons and through woodland, most of them very muddy.

Refreshments The Woodman, Lower Ashtead (180586).

It's astonishing to find ancient woods and common land surviving unscathed so near London, but here between Ashtead and Epsom they do. This walk steers you through the maze of footpaths that cross them, gives you glimpses into medieval farming practices long abandoned, and brings you face to face with the source of Epsom Salts, those settlers of nearly four centuries of morning-after tummies.

From Ashtead station (180590) cross the line. Woodfield Road bends immediately left; walk ahead here ('Ashtead Common' sign and blue arrow bridleway fingerpost) to cross a footbridge over The Rye stream (180593). Three wide paths diverge here – take the right-hand one (there's a narrow path further to the right that runs into trees, but ignore this) between blue-tipped posts across bushy Ashtead Common and in among the trees.

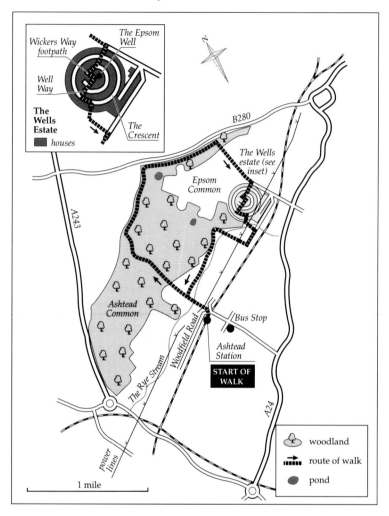

Here, north of the North Downs, chalk gives way to London clay, making all paths sticky and slippery. The Romans baked the clay into tiles in the brick-works they built on Ashtead Common, and in medieval times fish ponds were dug in the impermeable clay. Local farmers of the Middle Ages managed the forest that grew up on the common, pollarding the great oaks for firewood 10 feet above the ground to ensure that the new shoots were out of nibbling reach of the pigs, cattle and sheep that grazed the grass and acorns on the forest floor.

The woodland of Ashtead Common is dotted with enormous, centuries-old oaks, unpollarded for so many years that their shooting branches have grown into massive, twisted limbs stretching out and up from swollen, gnarled trunks. The common has been designated a Site of Special Scientific Interest because of its ancient trees, its nightingales and woodpeckers, its purple emperor and purple hairstreak butterflies and comprehensive woodland flora. Nowadays it is administered, like Burnham Beeches in Buckinghamshire (see Walk No. 7), by the Corporation of the City of London, and managed as a community woodland, with local people carrying out the pollarding and coppicing that have been revived after decades of neglect.

Where the trees end (176605) turn right ('Epsom Common' blue arrow bridleway fingerpost) and walk under the boughs of the outermost trees for ½ mile to reach the B280 (182612). Turn right, keeping just inside the trees, for a long ½ mile, to turn right opposite a road (192610 – 'The Wells' fingerpost) through the trees and across Epsom Common – another wild, bushy place – to reach a road (194602). Turn right here into The Wells housing estate, past shops and the top of The Crescent, and at the end of the cul-de-sac turn left down Wickers Way footpath to reach the Epsom Well (192600).

The well stands at the centre of The Wells estate's circular swirl of roads that were laid out in the 1930s. Recently renovated, the cylindrical brick well surround has been given a smart metal cover housing a lantern globe, and an ornate grille over the waters within. 'The Epsom Well', says the inscription on the slate lip, 'the medicinal waters that in the 17th century made Epsom the first spa town in England and a great resort and famous throughout Europe.'

This is no hyperbole. Epsom fattened and prospered on the visitors – Samuel Pepys, Nell Gwynne and George IV among them – who flocked here. By the Prince Regent's day the old well had long since fallen into disuse, the focus of entertainment having shifted a mile to the east, to the balls and junketings in the fashionable town of Epsom. But it was on this spot that Henry Wicker dug a water hole in the drought summer of 1618, and noticed that his cattle were refusing to drink the bitter-tasting water. It was infused with magnesium sulphate, distasteful to right-thinking cows but ideal for sufferers from gout and liver disorders. Bottled, the water sold by the million units – evaporated, it produced the famed Epsom Salts.

By the early 18th century the well was drying up through over-use. In 1754 a local apothecary, one Dr Livingstone, opened a new one, but it was a sham, with no medicinal properties. The original well, founder of Epsom's fortunes, stood unvisited and largely forgotten, until its recent refurbishment. But you still can't drink the water – the grille over the well is firmly fixed in place.

Walk down the steps of the well and turn right, left, then right again to the end of Well Way; turn left here, then first right and

through a metal barrier at the end of a cul-de-sac, to cross a stream (190598) and turn left on a path across the common. Fifty yards before the railway embankment bear right, and in 150 yards (190596 – beside a pedestrian crossing of the railway) turn right under power lines to cross The Rye stream (188599). In another 100 yards the path swings right; turn left here under the trees for ¼ mile. At a gate on the right turn left (183597), then right along a path between the wood and houses. Where the trees end, turn right (179594) to return to Ashtead station.

48

From Guildford to Woking
along the River Wey
(Surrey)

INFORMATION

Map OS 1:50,000 Landranger Sheet 186 'Aldershot and Guildford'.

Travel

TRAIN (BR) – Guildford (London Road) station.

CAR – M25 to Jct 10; A3 to Guildford. Park near London Road station.

BUS – Green Line (Victoria) 081 668–7261. Local information: 081 541–9639. Outward: London Victoria–Guildford North BR station. Return: Woking BR station (town centre side)–London Victoria.

Length of walk 8 miles – linear – Guildford (London Road) station to Woking station, and return by train.

Conditions Riverside paths – very muddy after heavy rain.

Refreshments The White Hart, Old Woking.

Between Guildford and Woking the River Wey runs through a lush and carefully tended landscape, in which mills, locks, bridges and narrow-boats blend pleasantly with pollarded willows and wide green meadows. This stretch of the river, and some of the surrounding countryside, is owned by the National Trust, which explains its well-groomed look. There's none of the dilapidation so often seen along canalised rivers that have ceased to carry commercial traffic - no broken lock gates, no scummy weirs and shabby warehouses. The Wey and its countryside sparkle like a new pin.

William Cobbett, that great 19th-century horseback traveller and scourge of politicians and other exploiters, rated the town of Guildford 'the prettiest . . . the most agreeable and the most happy-looking that I ever saw in my life.' Certainly the older part of the corn, cattle and cloth town that he knew is still attractive, with its solid Georgian architecture and Norman castle keep. The dominating red block of the 1930s cathedral is . . . well . . . noticeable.

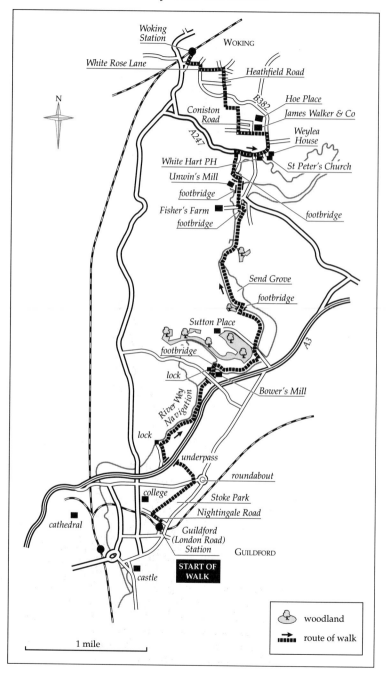

Woking Station
Woking
White Rose Lane
Heathfield Road
B382
Hoe Place
Coniston Road
James Walker & Co
A247
Weylea House
White Hart PH
St Peter's Church
Unwin's Mill
footbridge
Fisher's Farm
footbridge
footbridge
N
Send Grove
footbridge
Sutton Place
A3
footbridge
lock
Bower's Mill
River Wey Navigation
lock
underpass
roundabout
college
Stoke Park
cathedral
Nightingale Road
Guildford (London Road) Station
GUILDFORD
START OF WALK
castle

1 mile

🌳 woodland
▄▄➤ route of walk

From London Road station (002500) climb the footpath up the bank behind the station and bear left into Nightingale Road; then in 300 yards turn right at a gatehouse (001503) on a tarmac path through the grounds of Stoke Park technical college to reach the A25 (008509). Bear right to cross the busy road by the roundabout on to a path that reaches the A3 (004512). Bear left to go through the underpass and follow a stream to turn right along the River Wey's right bank (002516) in open country.

The lock here makes a beautiful picture – delicately arched iron footbridge, white-tipped lock gate bars, yellow brick lock-keeper's cottage, an island of alders, moored narrow boats decorated with traditional castles and roses. It only needs a frame and a signature in the bottom corner.

The Wey Navigation to London was opened in 1653, an improvement of the river with locks, weirs, short cuts and strengthening of banks and river-bed. Guildford's trade had been in decline for decades, owing to the bad roads into the town, but the canal gave commerce a boost. Horse-drawn barges plied the river until well into this century, but modern road and railway competition killed them off.

The path winds on by the river for 1½ miles to reach the lock at the handsomely restored Bower's Mill (012529). Cross the lock gates and a footbridge to continue along the left bank of the Wey around the woodlands of Sutton Place.

This big Tudor mansion (012536 – hidden by trees) was built by Sir Richard Weston; and it was his descendant, another Sir Richard, who backed the Wey Navigation venture in the following century. Sir Richard died before the works were finished, leaving his son George to cope – a poisoned chalice, since finances were so shaky that poor George found himself in a debtor's prison within six months.

Continue along the river to cross a footbridge (017540) below the charming huddle of farm, house and church at Send Grove, and walk on up the right bank past two more locks for 1¼ miles to a footbridge (017559), where you cross the Wey Navigation and keep straight ahead to cross a stream at the foot of a gravel drive leading to the medieval Fisher's Farm (013559). Turn right along the stream over another footbridge (016562) to reach Unwin's mill (015565).

In this splendid old brick mill Unwin Bros established their Saint Martha Printing Works in 1896, and the firm is still in business in the same building – a rare state of affairs these days.

Pass the corner of the mill and cross the mill pond to pass through a wooden fence at a bend in the drive (015566) and bear right along the stream to the A247. Turn right here into Old Woking.

Half an hour's exploration is time well spent here. Old Woking contains the superb Norman church of St Peter (021569), and beyond it the three-storey, Georgian red-brick Weylea House. Local legend says that Sir Edward Zouch of nearby Hoe Place ordered the third storey to be added to Weylea House to block out his view of the church, with whose vicar he had quarrelled.

Follow the B382 round a bend (021570), and in 300 yards turn left beside the premises of James Walker & Co (021572 – footpath sign), past shops and houses to turn right up Coniston Road (016572). A narrow lane winds north to a road (012579) across which you climb a bank and walk up Heathfield Road for ½ mile. At the T-junction (012584) turn left for ¼ mile, then right up White Rose Lane (008584) to reach Woking station at the top of the rise (007587).

49

Chobham Common
and Burrow Hill
(Surrey)

INFORMATION

Map OS 1:50,000 Landranger Sheet 175 'Reading and Windsor'.
Travel
> TRAIN (BR) – Longcross (NB There is no car park at this
> station).
> CAR – M25 to Jct 11; go right, then right again at first
> roundabout on A320 towards Chertsey; left in ¾ mile on
> B386 for 3½ miles to Longcross. Park at Longcross car
> park on left (979651).

Length of walk 6 miles – circular – start and finish at Longcross
station (if travelling by train); Longcross car park (if travel-
ling by car).
Conditions Heathland bridleways and tracks, often very muddy.
Bring a compass to help with direction-finding on the heath.
Refreshments Four Horseshoes or Cricketers, Burrow Hill.

The wild heathland of Chobham Common is one of the largest expanses of unspoiled lowland heath in southern England, a remnant
of a wide belt of inhospitable country that daunted pre-motor car
travellers. These days it lies open for the delight of riders and walkers,
a plunge into solitude. A contrast to this moody landscape comes at the
charming village of Burrow Hill, with a broad village green as its focal
point.

**From the platform at Longcross station (980660) go through the
white picket gate and turn right along the path round the perimeter of an M.O.D. research establishment. The path soon joins a
road, which you follow to a roundabout (978653); go straight over
to cross the M3 motorway, bearing left for 100 yards to cross the
B386 into Longcross car park (979651).**
   If travelling by car, start the walk here.

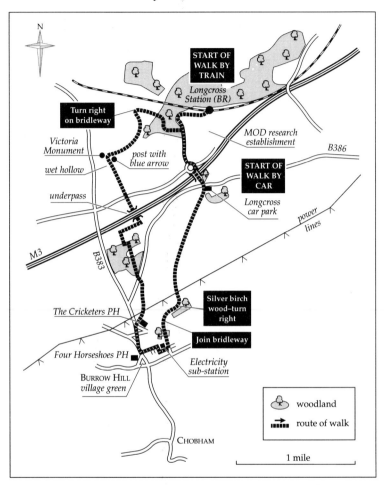

N

START OF
WALK BY
TRAIN

*Longcross
Station (BR)*

**Turn right
on bridleway**

*Victoria
Monument*

*post with
blue arrow*

wet hollow

underpass

*MOD research
establishment*

B386

START OF
WALK BY
CAR

*Longcross
car park*

*power
lines*

M3

B383

The Cricketers PH

**Silver birch
wood–turn
right**

Join bridleway

Four Horseshoes PH

*Electricity
sub-station*

BURROW HILL
village green

CHOBHAM

🌳 woodland
➡ route of walk

1 mile

**From the car park, a bridleway runs into the wide spaces of
Chobham Common, forking right in 100 yards to descend and run
south along the shallow valley of Albury Bottom.**

The sombre colours of heathland – dull browns, dark greens, ochre and
purple – stretch to the horizon in all directions. The sandy, gravelly
soil is patched with heather and bracken, freckled with the butter-
yellow flowers of gorse and broom. Silver birch, pine, fir, spruce and
scrubby oaks are widespread. Tracks run off at all angles over this harsh,
prickly landscape where the roar of the M3 soon dies to a whisper. 'A
vast tract of land given up to barrenness,' commented Daniel Defoe in
1724, 'horrid and frightful to look upon, not only good for little, but
good for nothing.'

But today's wanderer over Chobham Common, in no danger of being robbed by footpads or having to spend a night on the open heath, can rejoice in the solitude and the abundance of wildlife that the common supports. Here are foxes, squirrels, badgers, rabbits, roe deer, voles, 300 species of spider, 30 of butterflies, more than 20 of dragon-flies, 200 of bees and wasps; hobbies hunting the heath, and nightjars crouching in their ground-level scrapes in one of their few remaining refuges in England.

Long may the developers be kept away from Chobham Common.

Keep forward past side tracks and over crossings for a mile, to a rise of ground where several tracks meet (974639). The bridleway diminishes to a narrow track which keeps the same direction to go under power lines. One hundred yards beyond, turn right along the edge of a silver birch wood, and in a muddy ¼ mile bear left along a bridleway to reach a road between a factory and an electricity sub-station (973630). Turn right and walk down to the B383 at Burrow Hill (970630).

Burrow Hill's handsome old houses are scattered around the edge of the wide central common, a picturesque sight after the sombre miles of heath. The village pump stands on the green, and further down are Suttons' village stores (delectable home baking) and Chobham Forge where the blacksmith shoes horses for the myriad riders of Surrey.

Turn up the B383 past the turning to The Steep and Sparrow Row, and in 150 yards pass The Cricketers pub. Ignore the tempting green footpath fingerpost immediately beyond the pub, and turn right in another 10 yards at a wooden fingerpost (970633), cross-ing a heath to a driveway (971639). Turn left to cross a road (blue arrow) and continue north, following blue arrows as you climb through woodland and descend to turn right (968646), then left to go under the M3 motorway (970647). Keep forward to cross the B386 (969650) and continue northwards across Chobham Common for ½ mile, descending into a wet hollow and climbing gently to the crest of a knoll (post with blue arrow). Just to your left is the Victoria Monument (965655).

The granite monument, shaped like a plain Celtic wheel-cross, was put up just after Queen Victoria's death in 1901 to glorify her 'noble life', and to commemorate her review of 8,129 troops on Chobham Common in June 1853. This was the first military camp to be held on the common, considered useless until then. The Queen's 1853 review was the twinkle in the eye that heralded today's all-pervasive military presence on the Surrey heathlands.

Turn right at the post with the blue arrow, on a track that bears just north of east at first, then swings north. One hundred and fifty yards short of the railway you turn right along a bridleway (970661 approximately) which enters trees, swinging briefly south before turning east again to meet the M.O.D. establishment's perimeter road (976658). Turn left for the station, right for the M3 crossing and Longcross car park.

50

Pirbright
and Pirbright Common
(Surrey)

INFORMATION

Map OS 1:50,000 Landranger Sheet 186 'Aldershot and
   Guildford'.
Travel
   CAR – M25 to Jct 11; A320 to Woking; A324 to Pirbright.
      Park on village green.
   BUS – Green Line (Victoria) 081 668–7261. Local informa-
      tion: 081 541–9369. London Victoria–Guildford–Pirbright
      village green.
Length of walk 5 miles – circular – start and finish on Pirbright
   village green.
Conditions Woodland paths, some muddy.
Refreshments White Hart or Cricketers, Pirbright.

Visit the grave of Henry Morton Stanley ('Dr Livingstone, I presume?')
before walking deep in glorious woodland across some characteristic
Surrey heathland – fine silver sand that supports a wide variety of
wildlife. The rattle of guns from the military ranges on the heath only
heightens the sense of peaceful isolation on the tree-lined brink of
Henleypark Lake.

**Go down Church Lane (945559) to reach the Church of St Michael
and All Angels (942559).**

The smart houses of Pirbright stand round an enormous village green
lined with fine horse chestnut trees. The pear tree on the village sign
refers to Pirbright's name – '*pyrige frith*', the wood of pear trees. (You'll
look in vain for these in the woods around Pirbright today).

   The church was rebuilt in classic Georgian style in 1784, with tall
round-topped windows in the brick-walled nave. The west end has a
big gallery, and on the walls are many memorials to local young men
who died in wars from India to Flanders.

   A brass on the north wall commemorates Sir Henry Morton Stanley

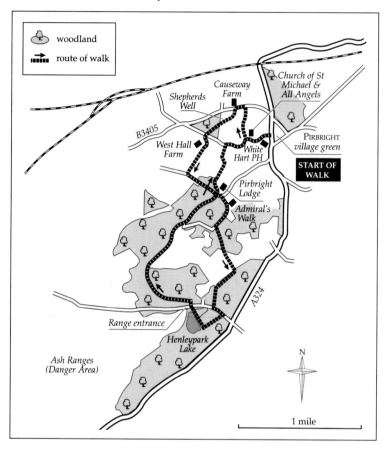

– 'He discovered Livingstone and revealed the sources of the Nile
& Congo, & was the means through Providence of crushing slavery,
introducing civilisation into central Africa & the first Christian
missionaries into Uganda.'

A great man, but one who had a number of hurdles to jump. Born
John Rowlands in 1841 in the Vale of Clwyd, North Wales, he took
the name of Stanley from the family who looked after him when he
arrived penniless in America, having run away at the age of 13 from the
workhouse in which he had been placed. Stanley became a hard-nosed
journalist, his greatest scoop the discovery of the 'lost' missionary
David Livingstone at Lake Ujiji, Tanganyika, in October 1871.

Honours flowed in on Stanley – he was knighted, and in 1898 came
to live at Furze Hill near Pirbright, where he died in 1904. His request
to be buried next to Livingstone in Westminster Abbey having been
turned down, Stanley was buried in Pirbright churchyard. His grave is
near the western end, a great slab of Dartmoor granite enclosed by a

little yew hedge and inscribed with his name and dates, his African name of Bula Matari, and the single, eloquent word 'AFRICA'.

Turn right out of the lychgate, and right again at the corner of the churchyard (footpath fingerpost) to follow a path up to the B3405 (942563). Turn left, and left again in 200 yards opposite Causeway Farm down a lane. Opposite Shepherds Well bungalow the track swings left (939561), but keep ahead here on a path through trees to cross a road and enter the drive to West Hall Farm (937560). Go between barns and through a gate into a green lane; in ¼ mile turn left (934554), and in 250 yards right along a tarred drive to a meeting of paths at Pirbright Lodge (939551).

Outside the Lodge gateway turn right up a track labelled 'Admiral's Walk', the name of the big timber and brick house you soon pass on the left. Three hundred yards on, bear left at the foot of a slope (938548) under handsome sweet chestnut trees and through a rhododendron alley. At the wood's edge cross a stream, a stile and a field into more woodland, over a culverted stream to turn right at a T-junction (940542 – blue arrow) and walk for ⅓ mile to turn left on a road (938537). One hundred and fifty yards short of the A324 go right (footpath fingerpost) through a conifer plantation, then right again (935535) to cross the end of Henleypark Lake.

This is a beautiful, tranquil spot, a big sheet of calm water encircled by heathland trees – conifers of all sorts, silver birch, oak, sweet chestnut, clumps of rhododendron – and fringed with sedge clumps from which duck and moorhens call.

Keep ahead at the end of the lake, and in 100 yards go right over a ditch. Pass the entrance to Ash Ranges with its warning flags, and in 30 yards go left just before a kissing gate (934539) onto a track through the woods.

The crackle and pop of small-arms fire echoes from the ranges during firing. The army has been here since before the Great War, having bought up large sections of the arid, unproductive heathland for training. The soil of Pirbright Common lies thinly on deep beds of sand, useless for agriculture but wonderfully productive – as you will have noticed – of silver birch, gorse, heather, bracken and bilberry, all plants that can thrive in these dry, acidic conditions.

Follow the track for just over a mile back to Pirbright Lodge. Turn left here, and in 50 yards right (footpath fingerpost) to a stile at the edge of the trees. Follow yellow arrows over fields and across a stream (939557) to the road (939558); turn right here for the church and Pirbright village.

51

Finchampstead Ridges,
the Blackwater River and Ambarrow
(Hants/Berks border)

INFORMATION

Map OS 1:50,000 Landranger sheet 176 'Reading and Windsor'.
Travel
  TRAIN (BR) – Crowthorne.
  CAR – M25 to Jct 12; M3 to Jct 4; A321 north; 2 miles
    beyond Sandhurst railway station, turn right at round-
    about towards Crowthorne; station is 150 yards along on
    right. Park at station.
Length of walk 5 miles – circular – start and finish at
  Crowthorne station.
Conditions Woodland, field and riverside paths. Bring
  binoculars for the bird life on the Blackwater Valley's gravel
  pit lakes.
Refreshments Waterloo Hotel, 100 yards from Crowthorne
  station (other pubs in Crowthorne).
Reading *The Three Castles Path booklet* (Ramble No. 4),
  available from Pat Hayers, 16 Lanterns Walk, Farthingales,
  Maidenhead, Berks SL6 1TG.

From the well-grown woodland around Crowthorne on its sandy, heathy soil, this walk descends into the wide valley of the Blackwater River where flooded gravel pits have been put to good use – some for water sports, others as refuges for wildlife. The contrasting flavours of water and woodland spice the ramble, with an added pinch of nostalgia in the once immaculate, now overgrown and jungly grounds of the demolished mansion of Ambarrow Court.

From Crowthorne station (822637) cross the railway bridge to reach Wellingtonia Roundabout (820637). From the angle of the B3348 Eversley road and the A321 Wokingham road a straight, gravelly path runs north-west.

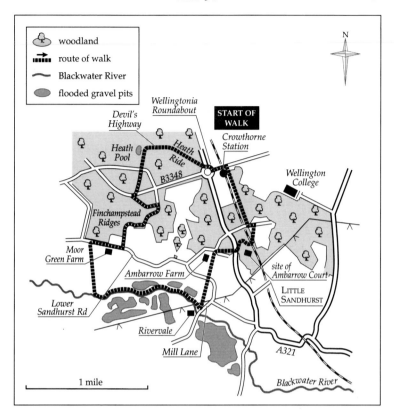

This track – Heath Ride – is well named. Silver birches and pine trees overshadow the path, and the bright yellow flowers of yellow loosestrife flourish among the blackberry bushes and honeysuckle. Here on the western edge of the great heathlands of Berkshire there's a strong feeling of dry ground and a sandy influence to the landscape.

At the gates of the Heritage Club (813641) bear left off Heath Ride past a National Trust 'Simons Wood' notice on a track known as the Devil's Highway. In 200 yards turn left down a crossing track (812641) which immediately forks; bear right here to skirt the left-hand side of Heath Pool. Turn left at the end of the pool for 200 yards, then right down a gravelly ride to meet the B3348 (811634). Go right for 50 yards, then left on a sharp right-hand bend (footpath sign) on a path between wooden fences. In 300 yards bear left beside a white-painted brick bungalow (812632), and in another 300 yards turn right on a track through magnificent oak and birch woodland.

The path meets Lower Sandhurst Road (810628); turn right past

Foxglade and Moor Green farms to turn left by a car park (805628 – bridleway and footpath signs) and walk down to the Blackwater River. Bear left along the near bank for a mile.

The Blackwater River forms the Hampshire/Berkshire boundary here, a snaking river in a wide, open valley that contrasts pleasantly with the enclosed character of the woods on Finchampstead Ridges. Greeny-grey and streaming with weed, the river winds past flooded gravel pits. Some are busy with sailors, wind surfers and fishermen; others with bird life – curlew, coot, moorhen, swans, snipe, mallard, Canada geese.

Opposite the opulent brick-built Rivervale ('Boarding Cattery – Danger – Guard Dogs!' – what on earth do the cats think of that?) bear left through a kissing gate just before Mill Lane (820620 – yellow arrow), walking north to cross Mill Lane and meet a road just beyond the old brick buildings of Ambarrow Farm. Bear immediately right at the road bend (821627 – footpath sign), with a fence on your left, for 300 yards to cross the A321 into a car park (824627) .

Paths lead off among towering pines and copper beeches and through tangled thickets of rhododendron to reach the grassy open space where Ambarrow Court once stood – a great Victorian mansion, whose head gardener would no doubt be appalled to see the havoc wrought by unchecked nature in his once perfectly tended domain.

From the north-east corner of the car park follow the 'Ambarrow Hill' sign for 200 yards; then turn right ('Ambarrow Court' sign) to reach the railway (826627). Cross – with great care! – and turn left over a playing field to a road (826630 – 'Ramblers Route' way-mark); turn left here, then right alongside the railway for ½ mile to reach Crowthorne station.

Windsor
Great Park
(Berks)

There are 5,000 acres of Windsor Great Park in which to wander, and here is a route through some of the best of them. A stroll through the heart of Windsor's attractive town centre in the shadow of Windsor Castle is followed by a good step-out along tree-lined rides and round ancient woodlands of magnificent trees, some of them pre-dating the Spanish Armada – the whole walk steeped in royal history.

From Romney Lock Road car park (970774) turn right along King Edward VII Avenue, pass Windsor Riverside station and turn left up Windsor High Street, following the curve of the castle walls with glimpses of the huge round tower that dominates the town. Some of the castle's finest apartments were gutted by the disastrous fire of 20th November 1992; a decade of restoration work will be needed to put right the damage.

  Pass Windsor Central station with its Victorian exhibition on your right and the pillared Guildhall on your left, and where the

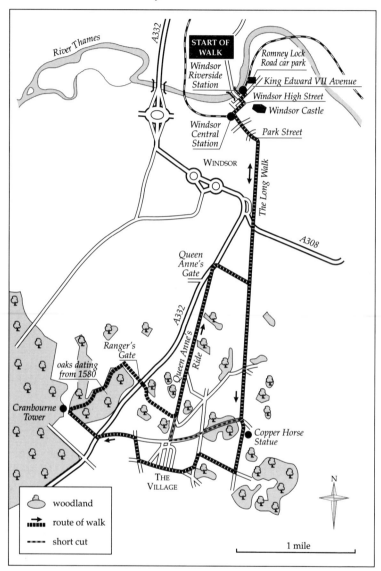

High Street bends right, go forward up Park Street and through the park gates (970766) to find the castle on your left and the Long Walk stretching away for 2½ straight miles.

The Long Walk was laid out from 1682 onwards to link the castle with the Great Park. The remnants of the great elm avenue planted in 1696 by King William III were felled in 1945 and replaced by the present rows of London planes and horse chestnuts. There are dramatic views between the gradually converging rows of trees, into farmland at first and then into wilder countryside where herds of deer roam. Ahead looms the enormous equestrian statue that closes the Long Walk.

The Copper Horse statue (968727) stands on a plinth of rough hewn granite 30 feet high, on top of a knoll artfully strewn with 'wild-looking' boulders. 'Georgio Tertio, Patri Optimo' reads the inscription, a filial tribute to the 'Best of Fathers' from King George IV, who had the statue erected in 1831. King George III sits astride his charger, cloaked and imperially crowned, pointing languidly away to the north-west. Green with verdigris and a perching-post for jackdaws, he and his horse still make a most impressive picture. But is the ensemble really big enough to have contained 16 men feasting on bread and cheese and singing 'God Save the King', as legend says happened to celebrate completion of the statue?

(✄ **Short cut – retrace your steps for 100 yards and turn left along the roadway for ¾ mile to the northern outskirts of The Village, where you turn right up Queen Anne's Ride.) From the statue continue over the hill and through a gate, to turn right in 200 yards and left at a road (961725), making for the houses of The Village clustering round their green (955724).**

In these neat houses live the Windsor Park estate workers. The Village was built in 1948 – the date is on several of the houses round the green, and over the door of the Post Office and general stores. Others are dated 1954 and 1966 to record further building. It's a suitably quiet and orderly scene; scarcely a leaf out of place.

Pass the Post Office, turn right at the road and left in 300 yards (952727 – 'Cranbourne Gate' sign). Note the oaks planted along here to commemorate Queen Victoria's Golden and Diamond Jubilees, and the coronation of her son King Edward VII. Cross the A332 (948727) and continue forward to reach Cranbourne Tower (942731), the remnants of a large building of about 1500. Most of the building was demolished in 1861, but Queen Victoria used the remaining tower as a 'comfort stop' on her drives in the park. Just before the tower, turn right with a wooden fence on your left and follow it to an opening in the trees with a view of Windsor Castle (948733). Bear right here to join a sandy bridleway through a wood planted with oaks in 1580 – many still stand, their trunks incredibly swollen and misshapen, their limbs lopped off by 400 years of storms. Where the trees end, bear right to cross the A332 and walk through Ranger's Gate (954734). Turn immediately left up a horse track, which descends from a wood to join Queen Anne's Ride (959730).

Queen Anne loved deer hunting. The Ride was planted in 1703, a nine-mile avenue from Windsor Castle to the Royal Kennels near Ascot where her buckhounds were kept. At the time of writing, conservationists are up in arms over plans to fell the storm-battered oak avenue and to replant it. An inspection of one of the weatherbeaten old trees will show the variety of wildlife each harbours – fungi, lichens, birds, spiders, gall wasps, ants, boring insects, squirrels, beetles. Yet trees become unsightly and dangerous with age, and new ones will grow to look just as stately. Should three centuries of slow development be done away with? It's a tricky question.

Turn left up the Ride (✂ *short cut* – rejoins here) for 1¼ miles, then right through a stile where the fence on your right ends at Queen Anne's Gate (964749) to rejoin the Long Walk and turn left for the castle.

APPENDIX

Useful booklets and pamphlets of walks:

Berkshire

Circular Walks and other pamphlets from Countryside Group, Dept of Highways and Planning, Shire Hall, Shinfield Park, Reading RG2 9XG (tel: 0734 234939)

Excellent *Rambling for Pleasure* series of guides published by East Berkshire Ramblers' Association Group (contact Pat Hayers, 16 Lanterns Walk, Farthingales, Maidenhead, Berks SL6 1TG)

Ramblers' Association Area Secretary – Mr J. Davies, Dingle Dock, East Garston, Newbury, Berks RG16 7HN

Buckinghamshire

Various pamphlets available from County Planning Department, Buckinghamshire County Council, County Hall, Aylesbury, Bucks HP20 1UX

Forestry Commission guide to walks in Chiltern woodlands from Chilterns Forest District, Upper Icknield Way, Aston Clinton, Aylesbury, Bucks HP22 5NF

Ramblers' Association Area Secretary (Buckinghamshire and West Middlesex) – Miss J. Jefcoate, 25 Willow Grove, Ruislip, Middlesex HA4 6DG

Hertfordshire

Information from Hertfordshire Leisure and Tourism Officer, c/o St Albans District Council, St Albans, Herts AL1 3QZ

Ramblers' Association (Acting) Area Secretary (Hertfordshire and North Middlesex) – Mr A. Richardson, 53 Green Drift, Royston, Herts SG8 5BX

Essex

Wildside Walks packs from Planning Department, Essex County Council, County Hall, Chelmsford, Essex CM1 1GG (tel: 0245 492211)

Countryside Footpaths series of pamphlet guides to walks in London Borough of Havering from Countryside Management Service, Directorate of Environment and Planning, London Borough of Havering, Technical Offices, Spilsby Road, Harold Hill, Romford, Essex RM3 8UU

Basildon Greenway Countryside Walks guide booklet from Basildon Countryside Officer (tel: 0268 550088)

Ramblers' Association Area Secretary (Essex plus London Boroughs of Waltham Forest, Redbridge, Havering, Barking and Newham) – Mr M.J. Haylock, 48 Symons Avenue, Leigh-on-Sea, Essex SS9 5QE

Kent

Wide variety of well-produced packs of walks, including *River Valley Walks, North Downs Way Walks, Greensand Way, Stour Valley Walk, Country Park Walks, Centenary Walks, Countryside Walks, Coastal Walks, Farm Trails.* Also some routes for disabled ramblers. Information from the Recreation Paths Officer, Planning Department, Kent County Council, Springfield, Maidstone, Kent ME14 2LX (tel: 0622 696168)

Ramblers' Association Area Secretary (Kent plus London Boroughs of Bexley and Bromley) – Mr B. Arguile, 42 Waldron Drive, Loose, Maidstone, Kent ME15 9TH

Surrey

Packs of leaflets including *Surrey's Countryside* (walks with themes e.g. Valleys and Views, Landscapes of Limpsfield, Smugglers' Trail, Trees and Timber) and *Walks from West Surrey Villages* available from the Public Relations Unit, County Hall, Kingston-upon-Thames, Surrey KT1 2DN (tel: 081 541–9082)

Ramblers' Association Area Secretary (Surrey plus London Boroughs of Richmond, Kingston, Merton, Sutton and Croydon) – Mr G. Butler, 109 Selsdon Park Road, South Croydon, Surrey CR2 8JJ

Ramblers' Association (Head Office)
1–5 Wandsworth Road, London SW8 2XX (tel: 071 582–6878)

London Transport
Tel: 071 222–1234